UPROOTED REANGS
STRANGERS IN THEIR MOTHERLAND

UPROOTED REANGS

Strangers in Their Motherland

SUBRATA KUMAR DUTTA

AKANSHA PUBLISHING HOUSE
NEW DELHI

AKANSHA PUBLISHING HOUSE
R 37-B, Vani Vihar, Uttam Nagar
New Delhi-110059
Email: ektabooks@yahoo.com

Showroom
4649/21B, Ansari Road
Darya Ganj
New Delhi - 110 002
Ph. : 23269193 / 9811582579

Uprooted Reangs: Strangers in Their Motherland

First Edition 2005
ISBN 81-87-606-91-6

[The responsibility for the facts stated, conclusions reached etc. is entirely that of the Author. The publisher is not responsible for them, whatsoever.]

PRINTED IN INDIA

Published by M.P. Misra for Akansha Publishing House, New Delhi and Printed at Tarun Offset Press, Delhi.

Foreword

India's northeast is now witnessing the second phase of the ethnic explosion. In the first two decades after independence, those who challenged the Indian control over this far frontier region were generic identities like the Nagas and Mizos. They fought and got- or failed to get - a deal within the Indian system that met - or failed to meet - their aspiration for an acre of green grass they could call their own. But while some of these rebellions continued, a new and more violent - and equally assertive - set of movements rocked the region. These were the movements of the smaller nationalities who were apprehensive of being absorbed by the large generic identities. The movement by the Reangs for their own homeland - in Mizoram or spanning across Mizoram and Tripura - is one such movement. Subrata Dutta's attempt to study the Reang movement is a laudable effort that would help us understand the new dynamics of ethnic politics in India's northeast. A close-up case study like this would go a long way to understand the contours of Northeast's second ethnic explosion - one in which Delhi is no longer as the only enemy and in fact is quite often seen as an ally to help achieve the small homelands these smaller tribes are looking for.

SUBIR BHAUMIK
BBC Eastern India Correspondent

Preface

The contents presented in this book spell out the most horrific story of Reang refugees. They are now homeless people, have been living in refugee camps since couple of years, despite having the status of Indian citizenship and staying for several decades in Mizoram in Northeast India. The aim is to draw lessons from the experiences of Reang refugees who were tortured, whose wives and children were gang raped, relatives were killed and houses were burnt.

This book captures all those communal disturbances faced by Reangs in Mizoram, within their own locality, from their very neighbours—Mizos, in the consequences of severe life threats, quit notices, forcible conversion of religion to disown culture and identity. Reangs didn't get any help from the government or any other organisation in that period of turmoil.

The facts presented in this book are the best examples of discriminations against minority Reang society, their long years of social and economic sufferings. They joined terrorism to combat such practices. The violation of their basic rights and the problems arrived out from there was the reflection of most progressive patterns of the conflict between Mizo and Reang tribes. Majority Mizos set afire at least 1300 Reang houses, damaging another 365 well-built houses and 30 religious temples in around 41 villages in Mizoram. More than 2000 people have died only in refugee camps and many refugees are still suffering in extreme poverty and health diseases.

Those incidents didn't get much exposure in mainstream media. I have, on various occasions, tried to bring the root causes of hostility of two tribes through various newspapers, but that attempt was not so successful, because of the crisis of space and time within media.

Then the idea came to capture the Reang refugee crisis in a book. Now I realise, my attempt to address the root causes of the conflict has been augured well and rewarded. Back in 1997, while reporting for a leading daily of Northeast, I witnessed this problem during a visit to the only camp sheltering Reangs. I began to introspect Reang refugee problem through a focused-study carried on behalf of Indian Institute of Human Rights, New Delhi. In the course of the study, I gathered crucial facts from various sources, held discussions with the victims, Reang leaders, interviewed several experts of this field and extensively visited various places of Northeast, from the early months of 2002 and during recent years, before publishing this book.

The tribal conflict is flickering more these days because of less attention towards tribal society. They have little voice and choice in functioning of the government, are denied right to resources, right to economy, right to religion and right to join politics. Majority community rules the government, governs state resources and its economy. Over the years, minorities were viewed as the backward people and hence discriminated from the jobs, education, development, health-care and other basic amenities. It, slowly but surely, led to the formation of terrorist organisations. There are more than three dozen terrorist groups active in Northeast of India.

This book focuses on tribal autonomy, inter-community relationship, torture, terrorism, human rights, constitutional safeguards and provisions for the minorities of Northeast India. Apart from all these, a wide range of measures have been discussed in this book to resolve the tribal conflicts of Northeast India.

SUBRATA KUMAR DUTTA

Acknowledgement

In the making of this book, I have got the immense support of my family, colleagues, Journalists, Reang leaders, professional experts, Academia, central and state government officials and officials of various NGOs. I have benefited from Shri Subir Bhaumik, BBC Eastern India Correspondent, Prof. B.K. Kuthiala, Dean, Faculty of Media Studies, G.J.U., Hissar, Prof. Buroshiva Dasgupta, Professor of Communication, M.I.C., Manipal (former Editor of *Financial Express*), Dr. Partha Chatterjee, Senior Journalist and Ex.-President of Calcutta Press Club, Dr. Biplob Loha Choudhury, Reader, Department of Mass Communication, A.U., Silchar, Dr. S.N. Bera, Reader, Department of Journalism and Mass Communication, C.U., Kolkata and Prof. Om Prakash Mishra, Department of International Relations and Coordinator of Centre for Refugee Studies, J.U., Kolkata, in various ways, often through a great deal of discussions and in receiving various materials. I would like to express my strong gratitude to all of them.

I am indebted to my colleagues Shri Uttam Shee, Senior Reporter of Dainik Jugasankha and Shri Sadananda Bhattacherjee, Correspondent of Assam Tribune, for making various materials available for this book.

I am particularly grateful to Shri Uttam Kr. Chakma former S.D.O. and Shri U.R. Debbarma, Deputy Collector of Kanchanpur sub-division in Tripura. They arranged my visit to the refugee camps.

Both Shri Krishna Raghunath Vhide and Harihar Prasad of Kalyan Ashram in Tripura helped me in various ways to understand the ground situation of Reang refugee problem.

There are many names don't figure in this book, but their contributions in this book are invaluable. Many Reang leaders who can be named, but for their individual interests, life threats and requests for anonymity, who asked their names not to be mentioned. I would like to thank all those people, Reang leaders and leaders of Mizoram Bru Refugee Committee for sharing their experiences of wrenching.

I would specially recall my Kolkata based friend Shri Subhasis Guha. He has shared a great deal of the burden of typing the manuscript. I am very thankful to Shri M.P. Misra of Akansha Publishing House for publishing this book.

SUBRATA KUMAR DUTTA

Contents

1 Introduction

All people have rights. Human rights in common parlance are the rights of life and dignity; in fact all rights – political, civil, social, cultural and others. These rights are fundamental birth rights which are enjoyed by all without discrimination of religion, caste, language, creed, sex or race. Concern for human rights has emerged as the single most important issue for mankind due to the activities of United Nations and increased awareness about human rights as well as the magnitude of violations of human rights throughout the nation in general and in northeastern states in particular.

The northeastern states are the cauldron of many tribes and autochthones. Though unidentical from each other, those tribal groups have their own language, rituals, customs, beliefs and perception. Religion pervaded in most of the tribal thoughts and values, made the people realizing the role of religion more profoundly. Thus, religion is the single most important aspect of those tribal societies, who live nearer to nature, and whose lives are largely influenced by its overwhelming forces. Religious faith as part of their life is simply interwoven in their socio-religious culture.

An approach towards religion is the expression of their inner realization, somewhat invisible supernatural forces controlling the course of nature, as it influences their minds and thoughts. The religion of northeast can be understood as a cultural imperialism, and in the pretext of cultural region.

Though their identity they interpret through their culture, social values, customs and language in their own way. Each tribal section has its own distinct religious culture and language, which they have retained over ages, uninfluenced by any other cultural trait. But in last couple of decades, it struck up by the influence of outsiders.

Vested Interest Groups

On the other hand, political and religious organisations are striving their goals. In great extent their dignity and rights have been hived off by those vested interest groups, and constantly they used to influence them for their own interests and purposes. In all that the minority tribes found to be in quandary and largely created a kind of vicelike feeling against other community.

Such insidious vested activity has created a messy situation in the whole northeast. Although, it is a difficult task to plug it further. Vested interest groups made their strong roots, making various promises to them for "tribal promotion", which ultimately had no real base in meeting the actual demands of individual and group tribesmen. Gradually this was progressing at a stage that was harming the entire community fabric and relationship.

Worstly suffered minority tribal groups in northeast have no other ways out; often look for some political shelter. The naïve tribes are easily allured by the propagandas of political and religious organisations. The tall promises of economic development, health care, education and employment were offered to them by two organisations, bringing outrageous results at last. The promises they make that hardly perk their confidence up. Extreme perplexity is the ultimate fallout.

That is why dishearten tribes are groping for identity, social, cultural, political and economic rights. The genealogy of human rights is suffered widely in most of the tribal society in northeast, leaving them with a giddy feeling. And, thus the inter- and intra-tribal conflicts and rivalry starts, only when they find the rivals guilty of the waning away fundamental rights. But this inspiration mostly come from political people. Various governments in the states, too, relentlessly adopted wrong policies and steps against minorities. Identity crisis and related issues are solely responsible for this current hostility and

insurgency in northeastern India. This is the most fate and unfortunate story of northeastern tribes.

Various political parties and religious groups are keeping them away from the mainstream of development. Helpless in such a situation, tribes are bound to live in most dilapidated condition. Deprivation is a factor which insisted them to battle. Continuous deprivation of the minority tribes is a cause which ultimately gave birth to 34 terrorist groups, now active in various parts of northeastern region, are fighting their democratic rights.

Tribal Resentment and Discrimination

In the growing terrorism, ethnic clashes, discrimination against minorities, unequal rights in politics and development that fraught with many perils, are escalating relentlessly day by day. We have never seen governments, political parties, religious organisations or any other institutions to combat such problems in northeast. In their hegemony they hardly had any fair approach to establish peace and even no such attempts were taken to bring social harmony.

Resentment within this tribal people is sparkling, because of the growing acrimony and religious antagonism. All round development without any discrimination is unthinkable. On the other hand, the majority community, who is holding the regime power, is also not giving any rapt attention to the development of minorities and even not underpinning their inner realm and democratic rights.

Since many decades, strong majority groups continue to bash small populated tribal groups. Along with that political leaders have a strong role to support such activity. For less opportunity in the states they languish under extreme poverty. These non-vicissitudes thinking, within the majority group, has largely forced the minority to take the path of democratic struggle. Encountering such discrimination may not be possible for small tribal groups, with their limited capacity, they can only churn out the idea of forming armed militant groups, as a measure to fight the discrimination, as they can only think of.

Consequently, more than 34 armed militants groups have made their strong base in northeast, operating since past several decades. United Liberation Front of Assam (ULFA), National Democratic Front of Bodoland (NDFB), formerly Bodo Security Force (BSF), in Assam,

United Peoples Democratic Solideraty (UPDS), in Karbi Anglong District of Assam, *Karbi National Volunteers* (KNV), *Karbi Peoples Front* (KPF), and *Dimasa Howla Dorga* (DHD), *Bodo Liberation Tigers* (BLT), NSCN (IM), NSCN (K) in Nagaland, *All Tripura Tiger Force* (ATTF) in Tripura, *Bru National Liberation Front* (BNLF) in Mizoram, few among them are fighting for their democratic rights. But, in common, it is the cause of "racial discrimination" and failure of exercising their "democratic rights".

More often the inter-community clashes which perpetuate, suddenly attack the villagers, destroying life and property. In internal community clashes in northeast, an estimated 157,000 persons of various ethnicities were displaced by the end of the 2003.[1]

Mass Influx

Northeast, a geographically and politically isolated area of India, is home to many "tribal" groups. Once sparsely populated, in recent decades northeast India's population has swelled with the arrival of millions of Bengali Hindus and Muslims from Bangladesh and from India's West Bengal state.

Population growth led to competition for land and jobs and unnecessary tensions grew within ethnic minority groups, as well as in-between migrants and ethnic groups. Those communal tensions gave rise to ethnic and politically based insurgencies that have battled the Indian armed forces, attacked each other, and turned on civilian populations belonging to rival ethnic group(s). The violence has caused widespread population displacement.

Though internal displacement in those areas is a fairly recent phenomenon, the origin of the conflicts that have induced displacement go back decades. Over the past 150 years, the northeast's population swelled from around 1 million to more than 20 million. In response to labour shortages in the nineteenth century, British administrators encouraged migration from East Bengal, and between 1947 and the present, hundreds of thousands of Bengali-speaking Hindus streamed into the northeast from what is now known as Bangladesh.[2]

Threatened by the mass influx of "outsiders," members of some indigenous groups established militant, secessionist organisations.

In the effort to establish their ethnic supremacy in certain areas, insurgents have attacked villages, massacred residents, and burned houses to compel other ethnic groups to vacate disputed territory, leaving the latter little choice but to move into ill-equipped and inadequately defended displacement camps.[3]

Refugees in India

By the end of 2001, some 500,000 people were internally displaced in India because of political violence, including about 350,000 Kashmiris and an estimated 157,000 others in northeast India. More than 345,000 refugees were living in India, including as many as 144,000 from Sri Lanka, 110,000 from China (Tibet), 52,000 from Myanmar, 15,000 from Bhutan, 12,000 from Afghanistan, an estimated 5,000 to 20,000 from Bangladesh, and nearly 300 from other countries. An estimated 40,000 Afghans have been living in India in refugee-like conditions.[4]

India is not a signatory to the UN Refugee Convention and does not have national legislation regarding refugees. The UN High Commissioner for Refugees (UNHCR) is present in India, but the government permits the agency access only to refugees living in urban centers and does not formally recognise UNHCR grants of refugee status. However, in recent years, a number of Indian court rulings have advanced the protection of refugees whom the government had considered to be economic migrants.

Migrants to Eastern India

Throughout northeast, conditions of the displaced remained poor during 2001 to 2003. Violence and displacement continued in some areas, and no intergovernmental or international organisations were present to help. Many of the displaced lived in public buildings and makeshift shelters, with little health care and no access to formal education. State officials and local NGOs provided some food aid, but the assistance often arrived sporadically, mostly insufficient. In spite of the Indian government's efforts to provide cash assistance and food aid to many of the displaced people often goes to wrong people.

Most asylum seekers fled to the eastern Indian states of West Bengal and Tripura, while others going to Assam and Meghalaya.

Numbers were difficult to obtain, and they are the regular migrants to India almost on daily, the Bangladeshi Hindus and Muslims infiltrate in India through various borders of eastern India and took shelter in India either in relatives' house or mingle with town or city population.

In Assam, Santhal, Bengali, and Nepali communities have been attacked by militant members of the Bodo tribe, who seek to claim majority status in the Bodo Autonomous Council area of western Assam, which was delineated in a 1993 agreement with the central government. Bodo resentment inflamed because of mass influx of outsiders - which turned Bodos into minorities in some areas of their homeland. Over 200,000 Internal Displacement Peoples (IDPs) now live in 78 relief camps in Kokrajhar and Bongaigaon districts of Assam. Conditions are very critical. [5]

Conditions of Displaced People

Few temporary sheds of polythene and aluminium sheets are made for their shelter. People sleep on the ground on makeshift beds of bamboo; and there is a lack of clean drinking water; and diseases such as malaria, jaundice, dysentery, diarrhoea and influenza often pose a serious threat. Groups of five to six people are forced to share essentials. To supplement food rations, which are adequate for at most 10 days a month, they are compelled to consume snails, insects and wild plants. Pregnant women, children, and the elderly suffer the highest health risks in the camps. Over the past couple of years, camps have been attacked repeatedly, leaving several dead and dozens injured.

Displaced Bengalis in Tripura are living in similar conditions. In response to the Bengalis' rapid attainment of majority status in the state, tribal militant groups such as the National Liberation Front of Tripura (NLFT) and the All Tripura Tiger Force (ATTF) have sought to establish autonomous areas by attacking Bengali communities. Bengalis are thus forced to flee to displacement camps which are poorly defended, as evidenced by the slaying of 32 people in a 1997 attack.

The official and much disputed figure of displacement in Tripura is about 28,000 people, mainly Bengalis. In Tripura it is estimated that at least 80,000 Bengalis have been uprooted from their home since the Left Front came to power in 1993.[6] More than 1500 non-tribal families were rendered homeless in 2000 as a result of attack by the tribal insurgent groups. Estimates of internally displaced in north Tripura vary, but Mizoram human rights groups estimated earlier that some 41,000 Reangs are being sheltered in 6 camps in north Tripura.[7]

Conflicts between Groups

In spite of government efforts to quell the long running Naga dispute, renewed strife between the Nagas and the Kukis in Manipur has resulted in the death of over 1,000 people since 1992 and found in large-scale population movements. Additional tribal tensions reinforce instability in the state. Kukis and Paites have clashed since 1997 and friction persists between the Nagas and Meiteis. Violent conflicts between these groups has reportedly left 50,000 people homeless as entire villages were burned to the ground.[8] Militants have also burned granaries, putting thousands of people at risk of famine and starvation. Eleven thousand people now live in displacement camps and the government of neighbouring Mizoram has restricted the displaced from crossing into its territory.[9]

Ethnic conflicts in Assam state have left about 5,000 people dead since 1978. Clashes between Bodos and Senthals continued even in the year 2001, resulting in 40 deaths. In early June, 2001 the region's minister blamed the deaths of ten forestry workers by the National Democratic Front of Bodoland general strike to protest the continuing presence of the Chakmas, whom they still view as refugees from Bangladesh despite the ruling of India's Supreme Court that the Chakmas are Indian citizens. The All Arunachal Pradesh Students Union called the strike to put pressure on the provincial issue and to deport the Chakmas.

In Mizoram, fearing persecution from the ethnic majority Mizos, around 52,000[10] Reang tribals fled from their homes during 1997, sheltered in north Tripura, bordering villages of Assam and the Chittagong Hill Tracts of Bangladesh. In order to accelerate the repatriation process, the Tripura government discontinued food rations and medical services in some camps, causing at least 2000 people starve to death. These IDPs died as a result of poor shelter and dirty water, and many reportedly became seriously sick. Additionally, displacement camps are susceptible to attacks and mismanagement. More than 31,000 Reangs (6,956 families) remained displaced in six camps in northern Tripura, they fled from neighbouring Mizoram in 1997 following attacks by majority Mizos. In August 2000, the Mizoram Chief Minister agreed to facilitate the return of the Reangs to Mizoram. By the end of 2004, the government failed to progress their repatriation.

Disagreement between the Governments

Disagreement between the state governments of Tripura and Mizoram on the number of internally displaced formerly living in Mizoram hinders a solution for the internally displaced population presently living in camps.

"The Mizoram state government claims to have completed the process of identifying the "legal" Reang residents of Mizoram and have placed the figure at a little over 10,000. With this, the Mizoram administration has literally rubbished the claims made by Tripura that over 31,000 Reangs living in the northern refugee camps belonged to the state. The announcement could have far reaching effects on the demographic profile of the region as Mizoram can now refuse entry to over 20,000 Reangs (Brus) who were claiming to be residents of the state. Placing the Reangs under two categories, the state administration claimed that while 10,142 refugees now languishing in Tripura refugee camps were the original residents of Mizoram, the rest had come from Assam, and parts of Tripura itself.

According to a state government report, while 8,396 Reangs were the residents of the Aizawl district, 1,746 belonging to the southern district of Lunglei. It claimed that the list prepared by the administration was based on records and not interviews. "Therefore, any Reang who could produce sufficient documentary evidence on his citizenship would be added to the list," the report said, adding that the administration had exhausted all means of identifying more people.[11]

The Indian government's response to displaced persons from Kashmir has been significantly different from its response to displaced persons in the northeast. From Babyal's point of view, that the Indian government spends 26 million rupees (U.S. $597,000) per month just on financial and food aid for the displaced. In Jammu and Kashmir alone, that has totaled some 2,741 million rupees (U.S. $62.9 million) since 1990. He claimed that the government has spent another 200 million rupees (U.S. $4.6 million) on compensation for displaced persons whose homes were burned down. The Jammu and Kashmir state government's policy toward the displaced is shaped by a high-level committee chaired by the revenue minister. He noted that the state government works in collaboration with the national government, "but as far as implementation of policy, the primary responsibility is with the state.[12]

Minority Discrimination

Adivasi which means an original residents of India and in northeast it refers to original tribal groups. Over 70 million people belong to *adivasi* tribal people in India, also known as scheduled tribes are commonly known as *adivasis*.

After independence in 1947, special provisions were enacted to protect the rights of *adivasis* including enacting special regulations to protect *adivasi* areas from encroachment by non-*adivasis* which included restrictions on purchase and transfer of land. *Adivasis* are also granted protection under the Scheduled Castes and Scheduled Tribes (Prevention of Atrocities) Act. Many areas inhabited by *adivasi* people in north-east were granted special status under the Fifth Schedule of the Constitution.

Most common in the friction between two groups is on community rights of *adivasis*. There is a great interest on land and resources has produced much complexity in the whole problem. A major issue of concern has been illegal encroachment by non-tribal landowners onto land traditionally owned by tribals.

Adivasis often do not possess land records and much of their land is communally owned, thereby facilitating challenges to land ownership. In many areas, the authorities have failed to act to prevent processes of dispossession and to enforce legislation designed to protect the rights of members of scheduled tribes.

In addition, as *adivasis* have traditionally inhabited many of the areas of India which are rich in forest resources has seen the process of declaration of reserve forests, has led to widespread displacement of *adivasis* who are reported to constitute between 40 and 50% of the displaced population".[13]

The unequal tribal /non-tribal and inter-tribal power relations have also played a major role in most of the conflicts. Northeast India is rather a geographically and politically isolated area of India. Once known simply as Assam, today the northeast is divided into seven states: Arunachal Pradesh, Assam, Manipur, Meghalaya, Mizoram, Nagaland, and Tripura.

In contrast to the main land of India, much of the northeast is sparsely populated. It is also ethnically more diverse: of the 430 recognized "tribes" in India, some 200 made their home in the northeast. An estimated 25 percent of the northeast's 31 million inhabitants are members of tribal groups. Also unlike the rest of India where tension between Hindus and Muslims is one of the prevailing socio-political dynamics, in some cases religion, culture, language and political powers are also the certain factors in ethnic conflicts in the northeast.[14] For example, Reangs and Mizos who have clashed in Mizoram are Hindus and Christians. Christian dominance on Hindu Reangs was a factor of the conflict. It is true on the other part of state government policies considered Hindu Bengalis as "refugees" from Bangladesh, while Muslim Bengalis as "economic migrants".

Social Ostracism

Diversity causes tensions within the region. Out of India's 67.76 million tribal population, 8.14 million live in its seven states. Some such as the Bodos are plain tribals while most are hill tribes. A few such as the Aka of Arunachal Pradesh are small in number while others such as Bodos, Dimasas, Garos, Khasis and Mizos are numerous. In three states they are more than 80 per cent and in one, two-thirds. But they are very few in the populous states of Assam, Manipur and Tripura. The Bodo-Kachari, a third of the tribals in the northeast, are only 3.7 per cent of Assam's 20 million population.

In Tripura the tribal population have declined from 56 per cent in the fifties to 30 per cent today. The 45 lakh [4.5 million] *adivasis*, whose forefathers were brought by the British in the 19th century from Jharkand to work in the tea gardens, are considered foreigners. Most tribes oppose their inclusion in the Schedule for fear that they will compete for the few jobs available.

Four states have tribals as their political leaders. But the towns where economic decisions are made are dominated by non-tribals, mostly from outsiders. As such emerge the unequal tribal-non-tribal and inter-tribal power relations and conflicts with the tinge of religious or cultural or economic or political autonomy.

Minority discrimination has taken a messy shape in the northeast. It delineates clear social strata, assigning highly structured political, economic, and social roles to each and every majority groups. Members of the majority group are expected to fulfill a specific level of interests in order to secure all resources available to them. While, minorities are viewed as separate or lower part of the system. Despite longstanding efforts to eliminate the discriminatory aspects in society, the practice remains widespread.

The practice of discrimination was maintained over many years, and still remains an important aspect of life. Many rural tribes work as agricultural labourers and majority of them are bonded labourers. They are among the poorest of citizens, generally do not own land, and often are illiterate. They face significant discrimination despite statutory protective provisions, and often are deprived of equal facilities for education and development as majority people have. In addition they face segregation in politics and jobs. Minority tribes tend to be malnourished, lack access to health care, work in poor conditions and face continuing and severe social ostracism.

It is reported that crimes committed by majority groups against minority, often go unpunished, either because of the authorities do act in favour such cases or because the fear of losing the regime power. However, in recent years, groups resort violence to protect tribal autonomy and rights.

In the provision of the Constitution our President of India has the authority to identify historically disadvantaged peoples and tribals. And can protect their rights taking appropriate action and providing them special benefits from special development funds, and special training programmes.

Low caste Hindus converted to Christianity marginally gain supports from Christian missionaries' action pagrammes and others, who are unwilling to convert, are suffering a lot. In some states, government jobs are reserved for majority people alienating minorities.

The Scheduled Castes and Scheduled Tribes (Prevention of Atrocities) Act of 1989 lists new offenses against disadvantaged persons and provides stiffer penalties for offenders. However, this act has had only a modest effect in curbing abuse. The NCRB reported that 25,638 crimes against scheduled castes and 4,276 crimes against scheduled tribes were recorded in 1998. This compares with 27,944 crimes against scheduled castes and 4,644 crimes against scheduled tribes recorded by the NCRB in 1997. However, human rights NGOs allege that violence against minority actually is on the increase.[15]

Minority Reangs

The Brus (Reangs) as the minority tribal group in Mizoram suffered the similar cause. They are the worstly suffered tribal group of northeast in ill-assorted government policies. The majority Mizos as well as Mizoram government have denied their social, political, cultural and economic rights. At one point of time they were forced to convert their religion. They were not allowed to follow their religious beliefs and rituals. They have no equal rights in the state, even were prevented to participate in development, in education, and in politics. This all had a discernible impact on Reang society. Comparing to Mizo society the development in Reang society remains tardy. Political parties especially state leaders timed the benefits of Reang struggle. Christian missionary, despite its strong influence on tribal group of northeast, harps on the class and religion elements in development. Mizo Christians are getting every facility from the Christian missionaries, while non-Christians have rare opportunity to ameliorate their social conditions, because of the less number of NGOs and other missionary assistance.

Reangs (Brus) are the pro-Hindus and lack equal rights in Mizo-Christian dominated society. When Reangs clamoured their political, cultural and economic rights in Mizoram, they coupled with life threats, their houses were torched, girls and women were gang raped, and were finally tossed out of Mizorm state by majority Mizos.

In Mizo religious bigotry, the question of Reang rights and autonomy is still baffling. Uncertainty is hovering around, no one is sure about it, when they will be repatriated in Mizoram from the refugee camps of Tripura. It is a sticky example of how minority tribal rights have been denied in Mizo dominated society. By and large, it is the common cause of many minority tribal groups in northeast, who suffer in majority yoke.

The knowledge of the similarities and differences among various tribal groups is one key to understand the cause of their rights violated. The rights of northeastern tribals and its violations must be considered as interrelated if we are truly to understand the tribal crisis. There is no doubt that the best predictions of some kinds of violation of human rights are merely the social exceptions of tribal society. Think about your own rights; what the facilities you have? What the political, social, cultural and economic rights you enjoy? Has anyone discriminated you in getting school and college education, and is anyone disturbing in your free exercise of your culture and religion? Are not you free to talk in your mother tongue? What would have happened to you if you were forcedly denied to access all these rights? What will you do to get all your these rights? Had not you occupied the better position than those of tribal groups in northeast? Would not you fight for the causes of your own rights, if denied? But we all always portrayed the better democratic rights through the constitutional framework. External factors act to determine the tribal rights at all levels of development may have negatively influenced some tribal sections or certain tribal groups.

These are the factors that forced most of the minority tribal groups in northeastern states to live in most dilapidated condition. This book will focus on the solution of the root causes of perpetuating violence amongst different tribal groups in northeast. Why do communal violence and terrorism take place within the northeastern states? How and why Reang tribes of Mizoram were uprooted and taken shelter in Tripura refugee camps? How the continuous discrimination against tribes has been affecting the community relationship? With what strategies the problem of internal displacement people (IDPs) can be manifested and how the refugees can be dealt with? How will you deal with repatriation process? Why the tribal rights and interests are necessarily to be protected? Answers to all these questions will concern us in the next few chapters.

Nature of the Reang Problem

The unequal tribal/non-tribal and inter-tribal power relations have played a major role in most of the conflicts in northeastern states of India. Self-determination, religious and cultural rights, economic empowerment, language and ethnic identity are some of the major determining factors in the ethnic conflicts in the northeast. Since long northeast remained a geographically and politically isolated area in which people did not have equal share in politics, economy and other development with the rest of the country.

Ethnically more diverse, northeast states withstanding of 200 recognised tribes made it their home. Tensions rifle in economic backwardness, discrimination and unequal civil and political rights and suppression of religion and culture. Such causes are the major source of the conflicts between Reangs and Mizos.

With that diversified culture and geographical entity of 200 tribal groups and some 175 different languages – northeast tribes are more concerned about their own distinct identity, separate language and autonomy. In search of their political autonomy and separate homeland Reang minority fell in victims in Mizo resorted violence. Mizos, to achieve full economic and political power in the state, have tried to rearrange the electoral balance by ethnically clenching their areas from Reang ethnic group, sometime targeting Reang communities which are actually be numerous in population.

In pursuance of political agendas, the state leaders in the ruling government had reportedly been supportive to majority Mizos. What is more worrisome is that the politico-religious organisations found to be responsible in the whole acrimony. Widespread discrimination is there even in providing development aids and social services to other religious group. Which some take the shape of communal violence.

The Reang (Bru) problem surfaced only when they propelled their democratic rights. With their unfulfilled demands, Reangs People Union (RPU), initially approached to the state government of

Mizoram with three points demands for including Reang programs in All India Radio, Aizwal; reservation of jobs for the Reangs in government services; and nomination of Reang representatives in the Legislative Assembly.

After 1990, Reang Democratic Convention started functioning for the preservation of Bru culture, customs, language and other socio-economic uplift in Mizoram. But the demands of the Reang autonomy, separate language and political representation could not get a place in Mizo society, that alternatively gave a feeling that Reangs are turning towards a separatist movement and this could pose a greater threat to Mizo society. Although, government opposed all. Reangs have not received any opportunity to exercise their fundamental rights in the state.

Being the minority in numbers they were oppressed by majority Mizo people. State government, instead of protecting their interests, disallowed their political, social, cultural and economic rights. Did nothing in fear of losing majority Mizo support. The lives of Reangs were trifle different in their homeland when government denied doing anything in their favour. The Mizo government, under the patronage of state Chief Minister, who in his political wit wandered into majority population and worked only for the well being of Mizo society and in rare occasion he served for Chakmas and Maras. That infuriated Reangs but they continued their peaceful struggle for their democratic rights.

In that stark controversy, Mizo youths (under various banners) started to prevent Reang demands and imposed peer pressure upon the Mizoram government not to grant the Reang demands. Many years passed in that un-dismissal dispute, Reangs finally became the targeted audience in Mizo society. On the other hand, political parties started reaping the huge benefit, by making Reang autonomy a major political issue. The pro-Hindu fundamentalist leaders actively supported the Reang movement in Mizoram. Taken them with Chakmas for joining this movement under same political banner. Mizo organisations strongly refuted this movement and branded Chakmas as "foreigners from Bangladesh" and Reangs as "outsiders from Tripura and Assam".

The Mizo organisations had made up their mind to toss out the Reangs with systemic plans and programmes. But it was not difficult too. To fulfill the Mizo agenda, they systematically cleansed the Reangs from Mizoram by nefarious activities. First, they started attacking on women and young Reang girls, forcing the Reangs to give up their Hindu religion and some of them were asked to convert into Christianity. Reangs who denied convertion had suffered in many deadly attacks, sometime torching their houses, ravishing women and young girls. Many were beaten to death and forced them to leave Mizoram. In most of the Reang villages in Mizoram, those innocent tribesmen had suffered in that Mizo mob attacks and no one seriously came forward to help.

Government was very skeptical to save their life and property. Those were the most sombre days that the Reangs had ever faced in their lives and it witnessed many such violations of human rights in Mizoram. Those random attacks ultimately forced the Reangs to flee from Mizoram with a population around 52,000. They sheltered in different states, few in Assam, some migrated to Bangladesh and Myanmar and a larger population took shelter in Tripura.

Many of the Reangs refugees became symptomatic at the time when they lost their daily food and solace. All of them became very weak, mentally and physically, finding no one to come around for help. Poverty and squalor immediately became a part of their daily life, until when started living in refugee camps. Green forests, tree leaves, cattle and snakes were their only source of livelihood and passing an animal-like life. Their lives subverted into permanent hunger and misery. That all continued up to two years initially after taking shelter in Assam and Tripura. Many Reangs who fled to refugee camps died of various diseases, without food, drinking water and medical help. National Human Rights Commission when recognised them refugees, they started receiving grants from central government. But that was too late. The initiative of the central government has lured Reang refugees, but that was not the permanent solution in protecting the lives and safeguarding their minimum basic needs.

Refugee leaders claimed that central grants did not reach to them regularly and sometime that grants siphoned out by local political leaders and government officials. Living in refugee camps is just among many of the insurmountable barriers. Concern was expressed that Tripura government is not willing to give any shelter to Reang refugees, thereby violating the basic rights of refugees.

Reangs are the citizens of this country. And even after the directives of central government their repatriation has not yet started. They are unlawfully detained in refugee camps, and languishing under extreme depression and misery, since last six years. The need of the hour is to overcome the present situation. If their rights are denied they may provoke a counter-movement against that government discrimination.

Government policies of IDPs and repatriation should not be meddled with politics and the vested interest groups only followed their political agendas. But the real problem lies on: will the Reangs be repatriated in Mizoram? Or, will they be settled down in Tripura along with already existing Reang tribes? The numbers mentioned by the Mizoram government that only a small portion of the Reang refugees were the citizens of Mizoram, that would not buttress the present argument on the Reang repatriation in Mizoram. The most bizarre aspect is that their quick repatriation is possible only when central government and NHRC take stern steps against Mizoram government or if they suggest their resettlement in Tripura. Next few chapters will glean and examine this situation more vividly.

NOTES

1. USCR 2001 p.157 & USCR 2003, India.
2. www.Refugee/articles/india.org.
3. www.Refugee/articles/india.org.
4. www.Refugee / articles/India.org.
5. www.Refugee/articles/india.org.
6. www.db.idpproject.org.
7. U.S. DOS, 2001 Section 2 d.
8. *The Hindu Frontline*, 4 August 2001, *Hindustan Times* 2 August 2001; *NPMHR*, 5 January 2002.
9. www.Refugee/articles/india.org
10. Bru Refugee Committee, Tripura.
11. *Internally displaced from Mizoram in Tripura:* www.db.idpproject.org.
12. Conditions for the Displaced. http://www.db.idpproject.org.
13. Amnesty International Reports, India. www.amnestry.org.
14. USCR January 2000, p.2-3, 5-7, Bhaumik, pp. 22-24.
15. Amnesty International reports, India.

2 Who are Reangs?

Reangs are one of the most prominent tribes of northeast India. They are an ethnic group of having the distinctive identity of speaking in their own dialect and share a culture sustained for centuries. They are recognised as scheduled tribe in the states of Mizoram and Tripura. They adopted '*jhum*' cultivation as their main source of livelihood as towed it the main passion for many centuries. After India's independence it transformed into several epoch-making changes in domestic economy, but the situation in the Reang inhabited areas remain unchanged. They are sill backward, isolated and uneducated.

Early existence of Reang was found in the Chittagong Hill Tracts (now in Bangladesh) and from there they migrated first to Amarpur sub-division in oversize population. Deb Barman traced their existence in Mizoram in Mayanithlong of Lushai Hills before their settlement in Amarpur.

Reang Society in Mizoram

They inhabited in 75 villages in Mizoram with a population around 85,000. In the relentless fear of persecution in Mizoram around 40 percent of the Reangs converted Christianity. The Mizo student organisations have no longer allowed them to carry their distinctive cultural identity. Some of them even asked the Reangs to change their religion and to change the names of the Reang children in Mizo style. Whacked by Mizos, Reangs have been maintaining a backward lifestyle in the areas of education, healthcare, employment and other social developments. Administrative department was too, maintaining an indifferent attitude against the Reangs. It was seemingly unbearable; Reangs rose in association to protect their identity, language, culture and achieve an Autonomous District Council under Schedule VI of the Constitution of India in the pattern of other minor tribes of Mizoram.

Their relentless transitional shelter sometime in coastal area or at river banks can be witnessed from their previous settlement near *'Karnafuli'* river (now in Bangladesh), in various internal conflicts have forced them finally to took shelter in Tripura and Mizoram. In Rajmal[1] it was mentioned that during the period of famous king Gobindomanikya (1660-67) the Reangs first toppled into Tripura. But the views are little obscure about their original homeland. The original homeland, according to Deb-Barma,[2] were Mayanithlong in the Lushai Hills now in Mizoram. However this disparity can not be claimed of denouncing their rights of citizenship in Mizoram, assuming their existence in Mizoram more than a century at least, they claimed.

The Ancient Reangs

Reangs are widely known as 'Tuikur' in Mizoram. Most of the villagers in Reang community prefer themselves to be called as Reang. In current years they are alternatively accepted them as 'Bru' which was attached with their language, trawl to get a strong linkage with hoary tradition.

Reangs claim their lineage to the mythical ancestor 'Bruha'. He was the oldest son of the Devtarani and Devalaxmi, born out of two hard stones erected by God. In his (Bruha) journey from Rangamati (Now in Bangladesh) to the Chittagong Hill Tracts (CHT), he halted at a particular point. From there, the Reangs migrated to Tripura and then to Mizoram where gradually some of them made their settlements[3] and permanent homes.

Karnafuli river was the strong indicator of the Reangs settlements in Mizoram, most Reangs lived on the banks of the river in Mizoram. This river is an important waterway in the hills and plains parts of the CHT area. They once used CHT territories and thereafter in the area where they live now. In Mizoram, Reangs have the settlements in the valley along the stream Lengai and Teirei which are the tributaries of the Karnafuli flows from the hills of Lunglei and also through Chimtuipui district before entering CHT and empties into Bay of Bengal.

Reang Heritage, Society and Culture

The Reangs belong to the Tibeto-Burman Group of tribes and in linguistic terms, they belong to the Bodo-group and are closely akin to the Tripuris. Reangs are divided into two major groups viz. Meska or Mechka and Marchhai or Malchhai. They were further divided into seven sub-groups. In the first group, there are seven sub-groups: (1) *Tuimaiyafak*, (2) *Mechka*, (3) *Mesa* or *Muchha*, (4) *Raichak* or *Raikachak*, (5) *Takh Mayakcha*, (6) *Waring* or *Wariem* and (7) *Charki*. The second group consists of: (1) *Murchhai*, (2) *Apet*, (3) *Nakhya* or *Nagkham*, (4) *Chamrong*, (5) *Darbong*, (6) *Sajraj* and (7) *Reang*.

Cohesion of similar customs, language, rituals and other systems can be traced in co-tribes and sub-tribes of the Reangs.[4] Mukherjee observed, ' the Reang clan is a consanguineal kin group based on the rule of patrilineal descent. It is characterized as 'Panji'. The 'panjihero' or clan structure seemingly assumes the form of a bisection of the community having two segments of Marchhai and Meska clans, and each of them apart from observance of communal ritual for the welfare of its clansmen, has economic and ceremonial obligations and it may be concluded that the Reang clans and sub-clans had political functions which is more important than the convention of certain social usages, which each clan had fulfilled. [5]

In present days, that obliterated under the influence of modern lifestyle. The clans have no more significant role in politics and social matters in Mizoram. The clans among the Christian Reangs do not regulate marriage, the Christian Reangs even though use clan names, which hardly bear that social significance. The traditional practice of helping each other in ceremonial and economic activities are still practiced within the members of non-Christian Reangs.[6]

The Pattern of Reang Society

From the very beginning Reang community have been maintaining a primitive form of governance to rule the society in certain direction for the well being of all people. Chiefs are being appointed to foresee the groups. In Reang society, all the fourteen sub-groups have their own Chiefs who are generally known as 'Rai' as its own Monarch who is treated as the Supremo and whose word has the great dignity and supreme in all matters. Like other tribes, Reangs have a traditional form of government. It is hierarchically based with 'Rai' as the head of the community.

The 'Rai' holds the key position in Reang society and his officials are made through selection. In ancient time in Tripura, under the rule of King, Rais were selected for the functioning of the government. A 'Rai' was the feudatory ruler under the king. In fact, the post of the 'Rai' was not considered heredity, after the death of 'Rai' others like Chapiakhan or in absence Chapiakhan next Chapia or next Raikachak was given the chance in commanding.

Besides them Rai had other important functionaries viz. the Jangchu, who was his Nazir, Darkalim, the priest of the Rai and the Dalai his peskar. The other members who were as official staffs were (1) *Bhandari* – storekeeper of the Rai, (2) *Kanda* – bearer of the Rai, (3) *Dugaria* – the second Drum player, (4) *Daor* – an assistant to the priest and (5) *Chhiakrak* – the distributor of *prasad* after *puja*. The '*Rai*' had a band of followers who are known as Choudhury and Ozhai.

It was like a federal government below central organisation, where Rai and his followers and assistants represent the highest authority in Reang community, apart from the existence of subordinate rules in each sub-groups of the Reang. In each of the 14 sub-groups of the Reangs had having one headman. He is sub-ordinate to the leader of the entire community but he is leader of the group.[7]

The Rai holds very prestigious position in entire Reang community, but presently they are no longer in that propensity and holds authority over the community after abolishing chief-manship in Mizoram during 1954. It is mentioned that Reangs have two parallel authorities which have the influence over the community, but that has created two different sects- Rai and Kachan. Kachan has become the rival of Rai, and also considered very influential, has ambivalent pattern of functioning as Rai.

The Role of Reang Leaders and Village Councils

The feudatory ruler is disappearing and the pattern of collective leadership is merging. In Reang villages new form of councils are chosen by the villagers. Persons considered wise and respectful are selected by the villagers as their leaders. Theft, adultery, divorce, breach of social rules and norms are the primary tasks of the village councils to deal with. Other functions include: construction and maintenance of roads and playground, mitigating disputes, allotment of *jhum* land and maintenance of peace in a village.[8] The village councils impose taxes Rs. 2 per house and Rs.2 per *jhum* plot.

During bygone days, Reangs have revolted twice against the yoke of the Rais, Kanchans and the Choudhuries, during 1940 and 1943. It was the revolt against discrimination within their people. Otherwise they lived together comparative anonymity for centuries, as sturdy and straight forward tribe.

From the beginning Reangs have the fear psychosis of sudden attacks from outsiders and it was the constant fear in Reang community. As a result they preferred to live on the slope of the hills or hillocks for a protective life, they believe, that cannot be easily attacked. Platform build by bamboos known as 'Tong-ghar' generally make Reang houses. The house roof is covered by sun grass corrugated tin sheets are few as the villages can not afford to purchase it.[9]

Gods and Goddesses of Reangs

The Reangs worship some spirits and at the same time Hindu Gods and Goddesses. The spirits are 'Abursumaw', 'Khungchuhkarnow' for good harvest and 'Tanluphuihmaw', 'Kebengbumaw' for the recovery from disease.[10] They pray to Gods and Goddesses in Hindu style deity '*Maitoikhaim*' is equated with Laxmi and '*Baroi Pointimi*' is with Kali. The goats and fowls are offered to Gods and Goddesses in the style of Hindus do. The pattern is followed during prayers to *Baroi Pointimi* (Kali), *Sainai Pointimi* (Kartic), *Toto Pointimi* (Ganga), Saraswati and *Satya Birimi* (Narayan). In traditional Reang family, they, on daily basis, attend prayers as we find in Hindu family.

Reang have special ceremonies. Before starting seasonal cultivation, every village people participate in this ceremony, most respectfully remember Gods and Goddesses before starting cultivation work. In this ceremony, fowls, pigs and goats are sacrificed. In Tripura, their religious practices are celebrated in Tripuri style. 'Bishu' is considered a major festival among the Reangs who follow the indigenous faith. It starts with the last day of Chaitra (according to Bengali Calendar), followed on first day of Baisakh or the Bengali New Year. It is a non-religious festival and anyone can participate in it. Even Christian Reangs most enthusiastically join the festival.

However, traditional culture and various religious practices are rapidly going to oblivion in Mizoram. Christianity inched closure to Reang society. Their conversion to Christianity has led them missed to follow their traditional rituals, instead they follow *Basikiti* (New Year Day), *Khrismas* (Christmas) and Good Friday.

Reangs believe, a person further born after his death. As like a common practice in north-east tribal society, Reangs too keep a dead body in the house for a couple of days and displayed for friends and relatives' last look. The dead body is washed thoroughly and covered with a new cloth. *Augchai* – the priest who sacrifices two fowls one is for the soul of dead person and another for the spirit. It is a ceremony called 'Maibawn', the people dance around the dead body. The dead body is placed on a funeral coffin made of bamboo mat. The family members, relatives and friends of the dead body, carry the funeral bier and proceed for cremation ground through a procession. In this occasion a function is organised inviting the people to attend the feast.

The Changes of Reang Society

Reangs are highly social and cordial, they always help each other in the society. They maintain a mutual understanding, even when man is in great trouble they extend their helps. They always share a concerted effort of building the society for the purpose of Jhum cultivation, construction of houses. In social events whole village people participate and even in economic and religious activities are attended by all.

Free mixing of boys and girls are strictly prohibited in Reang traditional society. But the present Reang society underwent into several changes, youths freely mix with Reang girls and has given the birth of many premarital pregnancies. This change in Reang society has largely taken place in Mizoram, where neighbour communities such as Lushai or Pang who allow free mixing of girl and boys.

Male is always welcomed in Reang society as for the matter of facts that he would be able to help the family for its economic growth by directly participating in cultivation and other domestic affairs. While women rarely participate in heavy works, their works involved with weaving, fetching fire woods, cooking, rearing children and other household works.

A Reang daughter cann't claim her parent's property. Even when a parent dies without a male off-spring, the properties are not given to the daughters who after marriage stay with their husbands separately. The Reangs are a male dominated society, women are treated second citizen after male. Even after their marriage they are not free enough to attend any social function; they have to seek permission of their husbands. To attend any religious function even they seek family permission.

Reangs are extremly fond of songs and dances, which are deeply rooted their tradition. *Mishami* is the name of a Reang dance in which most of the Reangs participate. It is further divided in two types: called *daito* and *goria*. *Daito* is a type of dance is performed at the worship of Laxmi while *goria* dance is performed when someone passes away.

Economic Condition of Reangs in Mizoram

Lack of industry, infrastructure and communication facility, the poor initiative in exploring local resources and high corruption in development are some of the vital reasons which forced entire northeastern tribal society to remain as isolated and backward. While most of the tribal societies living in much dilapidated condition, the situation is more sluggish in Reang villages in Mizoram. No satisfactory fund allocation is made for the development of Reang village.

Villagers trudge miles after miles to reach a market place for selling their products, the distance is at least 5-10 kilometers. Though no such economic activity rolling in Reang dominated areas, agriculture remains a major source of their livelihood. The method of cultivation still is a primitive type and hence insufficient production to manage their needs.

Jhum cultivation mainly depends on monsoon rain. They generally start working from December. Initial work starts with clearing jungles. Hill slope lands are their foremost choice for such cultivation. Through this cultivation they produce rice, cotton, vegetables and corn. First process of cultivation starts with selection of a site and undergo worship *Burachha* (the presiding deity of *jhum* for rice harvest). Preparation in the field is followed by sowing on an auspicious day.[11]

Land, forest, and water are the only three main resources on which their economy keep going. There is huge crunch in their resources. The only resources are forest and land, which are under the control of state government. A trend is in vogue, more and more lands are taken for reserve forest. This has created a messy situation in Reang villages. Besides agriculture Reangs also involved with the works such as carpentry, basketry, fishing, hunting, cattle rearing and labour work.[12]

Indigenous Rural Development Project (RDP) office does provide some sort of loans to the villagers for making of handcrafts items, production of vegetables and other carpentry and tailoring works. That is not sufficient enough to make them self-sufficient and self-sustained. Children under age engaged in agriculture and soaps rarely encouraged in education and self-development.

Reang villagers can't only depend on *jhum* cultivation, when *jhum* season is over, they suffer in great financial crisis. During that period they work as casual labours in various sectors. As casual labours, many of them associated with the department of electricity, public works department and forest, although fetching meager earning.

Another grave situation is the purchasing power. They cannot afford to spend money on any kind of communication media. Radio and television have been out of their reach. They can not purchase even a radio set. A scheme - *Anganwadi* - was introduced in Reang villages for providing biscuits and milk to the children in some villages. In rare case, rice and sugar are supplied through fair price shops.

Poor Social and Economic Condition

The Reangs in Mizoram are the poorest among all the tribes. The Reangs feel that their neighbouring communities are economically well off. Due to these reasons they place themselves at the bottom of the state rudder.[13] This has given them a feeling of fighting against the yoke.

In inchoate social condition and economic hardship they always searched for a better living condition equating with other communities. Much played in the hands of religious Gurus, religious conversion could promise a better future and healthy economy. It worked sound at times at least in Reang community but that attempt and religious sacrifice given them a halcyon lifestyle.

Apparently health and education infrastructures are very acute in Mizoram, especially in Reang dominated areas. Health centres have not yet been set up in the villages. They go with high risks during the time of women pregnancy or in the propensity of health diseases. Penetration of modern medicine is almost absent and they are totally based on the traditional medicines. They have the traditional form of doctors who attend the patient for treatment. Pure drinking water is out of their dream and even the electricity didn't reach in Reang villages.

Currently , primary schools have been set up almost in all villages, But boys and girls are not encouraged for enrolment in higher education. School drop-out is very high in the community. Most children in villages end up their education at primary level and engage in family works, many leave school before completing primary education. Resultantly, literacy rate is low and in this baffled education set up, this community has produced only four graduates.

Relationship with Other Tribes

Geographical proximity apart, culture and language which has made the Reangs maintaining an amicable relationship with Tripuris, with whom they lived together for many decades. In contact with Tripuris, Reangs have transformed into societal changes, bear a great resemblance.

In Mizoram, they came in contact with Lushais, Bawns and Chakmas. But that exchange of cultural traits with other tribes in

Mizoram has severally displaced their socio-cultural Identity. In contact with modernity and Christianity which has influenced a larger portion of the Reangs to accept Mizo culture. In trun, it has become a barrier in their internal relationship, while non-Christian Reangs still maintain their tradition and culture.

Politically and socially they are closely mingled more with Chakmas than other tribes. It can be cited here that for the reason of migration from same place (CHT), both tribes still believe Hindu mythology and hence remain as Hindus.

Within Chakma District Council (CDT), some Reang villages are located where they are in direct link with Chakmas, Pangs and Bawns. But many years of living together in the same community, intertribal marriages are taking place quite frequently and they are in close relationship with other tribes.

In recent years, the efforts have been made to integrate all Reangs, inhabiting in various places of Mizoram, Tripura and Assam. After swelling of the conflict with Mizos, Reang leaders exposed into greater contact with political leaders within states and central level.

In Tripura, they made a special headway in making close contacts with other tribal societies and keep abreast all tribal developments in the line of greater tribal autonomy. That means of achieving all democratic rights are at stake, the relationship with Lushai virtually came to a deadlock and pared down on ethnic conflict. A better relationship among the two is not achievable if the leaders of both sides do not address the current situation prevailing.

Reangs of Mizoram

Reangs having population around 85,000 spread to some 75 villages in the western part Aizawl district and some villages of Lunglai and Chimtuipui district of Mizoram. Most of the Reangs (80%) of them are daily wage earners and literacy rate within the community is very low.

By and large Mizos are educated and a developed community. They have the population around not less than 6 lakh. Mizos are the majority in members in the state and have their strong influence in functioning of the government and other functioning of the society.

Policies are based against the interest of Reang community. Politicians, government bureaucrats and other functionaries take the path of discrimination mostly reared by state political leaders and Mizo student union, Mizo Zirawi Pawl (MZP). This organisation buoyed the concept of discrimination against the Reangs, threatened them to confirm general culture and religious standard followed in the state. They wanted Reangs to abdicate children's name in accordance with Reang tradition and rename to the Mizo style of naming. Since the inception of the state, this process was followed in the entire state. This rephrased very strong punishment if not followed by the Reangs.

The President of India, under Article 342(1) of the Constitution of India, declared that there is a number of scheduled tribes in Mizoram. These include, Lushai, Hmar, Pawi (Poi), Ralte, Khiangte, Simte, Paite, Gangte, Thadon, Zou, Vaiphei, Reang, Chakma, Mog etc.

Under Sixth Schedule of the Constitution of India, Mizoram has three District Councils. These are: Chakma District Council, the Lai District Council and Mara District Council under Chimtuipai Administrative Autonomous District Councils. According to the norms, the district council can safeguard the customs, traditions etc. to protect the interests of the scheduled tribes living in Autonomous District. But there is no longer autonomous district council for the safeguard of Reangs of Mizoram.

In order to protect, develop and uplift Reang society the Bru (Reang) National Union (BNU) was formed in 1994. To pave the way of development in Reang community, BNU held a meeting on September 23-24, 1997 at Suipuilui village of Mamit sub-division of Aizawl. It was demanded by the *inter alia* that an autonomous district council under the schedule of the constitution has to be set up to protect their cultural identity and they also demanded for inclusion of the names of the Reangs whose names were discarded from the electoral register. It was intentional and learnt from the facts that with the possibility of protecting a Reang MLA who was supposed to represent the area inhabited by them. This infuriated the chauvinistic section among Mizos who felt that Reangs are not only occupying their areas but are also trying to spread their domination. This has given a vicelike feeling to the Mizos, who rose in rebellion and the Vice President of BNU, Lalnunzira Reang was brutally assaulted by the Mizos. This incident took the shape of communal antagonism, many Reang villages were ablazed, men and women were killed and young girls were raped. Leaders of BNU, Bru Socio-Cultural Association (BSCA), and Bru Student Association (BSA) were arrested and detained illegally by the government of Mizoram during the months of October and November,1997. The Mizoram Police (MP) raided the houses of Reang leaders and arrested them without any warrant.

In continuous torture and killing in Mizoram by the Mizo miscreants has forced the Reangs to flock into Hailakandi district of Assam and at Kanchanpur sub-division of Tripura, from the places of Bhairobitol, Lemmhuikon, Saihapur, Simlong, Mualthang, Tlangkhan, Lemuikar, Chubel, Saikati, Hrifaw, Tumpanglui, Bazirungpa Para, Luseicherra, Dinthar, Bawngva, Rastali, Tuipuibari, Serhun, Bunghmun, Hnahthialzawl, Phaizau, Bethani, Rajivnagar, Longmai, Boragar, West Faileng, Cherikvel, Korte, K. Sarali, Pathiontheng, Moncherra, Kolalion, Agarbasti, Balikhal, Dungkhal and many other villages in Mizoram. After many days of walking on foot apartheid Reangs, crossing high hilly terrain, mountains and river, reached Assam and Tripura. Left behind many people who fell victims of various diseases and died in uneventual adversities. The distance traveled by them was very exhausting and rigorous, carrying their infant babies on bamboo baskets along with heavy bag and baggage. But their traveling from the Reang villages in Mizoram to other states: Tripura and Assam still re-memories the struggle they waged during those days.

Reangs in Hailakandi District (Assam)

After their arrival in Hailakandi district of Assam, the situation had entangled their life; there were no formal camps where they could get little shelter. Some of them got shelter in their relatives houses (local Reangs) and others, who have no connectivity with the people and land, fumbled on foothills, plain grounds and nearby railway station called - Ramnathpur. Most unfortunate was that even they could not been accommodated in any school, there was no such schools available for them.

That has left them to arrange for their own. They tried to settle them on government revenue land. District administration did not further allow them to settle there.

They had no other opportunity to get engage in any work or to continue their usual livelihood because of unfamiliarity with place and people. None others, Kalyan Ashram, Ramkrishna Mission Akhonda Mondoli and some local clubs provided them rice, wheat and cloth. Administration of the Hailakandi district provided them 389 blankets, 417 mosquito nets and in five occasions salt and rice were supplied with a provision of 600 grams per adult, 400 grams per minor and 1 kg of salt per family. According to a government record, 1755 adults and 720 minors were given that rations. These rations were discontinued only after five occasions. The refugees came to the district on October 13, 1997 and government supplied the rations as on March 7, 1998 and continued upto July 14, 1998.

A doctor was deployed at that locality for their health check up. In regular attack of malaria and gastroenteritis, the single doctor ended up his task providing only two tablets of malaria. In absence of regular and proper medical checkup, that claimed many lives, Bru Natioanl Union (BNU) said, 381 refugees died in starvation and a large number of people died in various diseases.

Reangs too had suffered in Assam, because, they had no political representation in the state. And other leaders were not enough dedicated to place the demands before higher authority. Another problem was the regular threats set by the Mizo miscreants who continued torturing the Reangs at the sheltering areas of Assam. Six women were brutally tortured on November, 28, 1997. Mizos demanded that the forest villages of south Hailakandi district in Assam which was the part of Mizoram and they were asked to vacate the land. They were in the vortex of great insecurity and decided to move out for other places.

NOTES

1. K.C. Shing, *Rajmala*, Akshar, Agartala, 1997 .
2. Suresh Dev Barma, Tripura Adhibasi, *Jiwan-o-Sanskriti*, p. 40.
3. S.K.Bhattacherjee, *Reang People of India*, Seagull Book, Calcutta, 1995.
4. Suchintya Bhattacherjee, *Genesis of Tribal Extremism of Tripura*, Gian Publishing House, New Delhi, 1991, pp. 12-13.

5. *Reang - People of India, Mizoram volume,* Seagull Books, Calcutta, 1995, p. 157.
6. *Ibid.*
7. *Panchyati Raj* in Tripura with special reference to Panisagar community development block area, (Printwell, Rupa Books Pvt. Ltd, Tilak Nagar, Jaipur, 1993), pp. 35-36.
8. *Ibid.*, p. 40.
9. Suchintya Bhattacherjee, *op. cit.*, pp. 12-13.
10. S.K. Bhattacherjee, *op. cit.*, pp. 154-164.
11. Ibid., pp. 37, 38.
12. *Ibid.*
13. *Ibid.*

3 Historical Background of Reang Conflict

Presently, the Reang tribes are found in the areas of eastern India and Bangladesh. Primarily known as the primitive tribes of Bangladesh, but since last two millennia they bifurcated to several places in India due to the internal tribal ethnic clashes and livelihood. In India, they live with huge population in the states of Mizoram, Tripura, and Assam.

Reangs claim, they are the descendents of the mythical ancestor "Bruha",[1] who migrated from the Chittagong Hill Tracts (CHT) of present Bangladesh. They first entered in northern and southern part (Amarpur and Belonia) of Tripura and thereafter moved towards east (western part of Aizawl district, Mizoram).

The Reangs are one of the primitive tribes in the northeastern region of India. It is believed that being driven out by Mugs, they migrated to the east of Gomti river in Tripura from the Chittagong Hill Tracts (now in Bangladesh) in the middle of 15th century during the reign of Ratna Manikya.[2] They settled down in Belonia and Amarpur sub-division of the state.

A huge population of them can be found in their homeland – Mizoram also. They had been living in Mizoram for more than 100 years. The construction of Mizo language, and in its word repertory, has a larger influence of Reang language. There have been of many Reang words expressed in Mizo language. Mizoram is their birth soil and is also a motherland, claimed Bru Students Association (BSA) President Brunu Masa and G.S R. Lalbhang Liana of Mizoram.[3]

The two major clans – Molsoi and Meska (Mechka) further divided into many sub-groups. Uchoi (Husoi), Chamrong, Wariem Raichak etc. the prominent groups among them, are generally known as Reangs. Reangs are known as one of the sub-clans. They constitute the second largest population in Tripura. Reangs spread across several northern and southern sub-divisions of Dharmanagar, Kailasahar, Kamalpur, Udaipur, Amarpur, Belonia, bordering Assam, Mizoram and Bangladesh.

Reang Settlement in Mizoram

In Mizoram, they are located mainly on the western part of Aizawl district (bordering Tripura) and on the north (bordering Assam) with sparse settlements upto Lunglei in southwestern parts of the state bordering Chittagong Hill Tracts, Bangladesh, accounted a population around 85,000 scattered around 120 villages in Mizoram (according to Bru National Union's Memorandum submitted to Prime Minister,1998). The government of Mizoram, however, disagrees with this fact and made it unrealistic.

Reangs, live in a very difficult terrain behind their ordinary though hard life, and behind this they feel the interplay of natural forces playing their different and yet distinctive roles, devastations caused in each time, all unaccountable: the majority attacks come suddenly in spate, bash and ruins the whole village. Sometime this unnatural human attack forces them to move to different regions for living.

As a result of their regular translocation from one place to another, they had to face severe threats and sometime coupled with communal violence. The prevailing socio-economic conditions still find them as remote, backward and beast. Instead of getting help from neighbouring tribal society, they were suffered in social ostracism. Behind them there had hardly anyone stood and supported.

The instance of steady progress and all round development, when sparked off in other tribal areas in Mizoram leaving the Reangs in much isolation and deprivation, has opened their eyes. Being as the minority population in Mizoram, they were neglected from government jobs, education, community development and in many other areas. This raised frustration in Reang society. Though the government claims to have carried several programs in Mizoram state, but the progress is hardly visible in their areas.

Lack of Attention

Reang villages have got no attention in comparison to non-Reang villagers in Mizoram. They have not taken for any mainstream development, in education, healthcare, jobs and infrastructure building. As because of the minority in numbers they were oppressed by the majority Mizos. They had to live in a society where they hardly had any opportunity to earn and maintain the livelihood. And development is mare sheen in their society.

After having discussions with Reang leaders and social observers it has drawn the facts that the Reang problem spawned basically from a general perception of continuous deprivation and negligence of their culture and traditional values. They were the strong believer of Hindu tradition and they had to live in different socio-cultural system– highly influenced by Mizo-Christian society. That was, in some extent, unbearable and un-adjustable. Reangs' lifestyle, believes, feelings, cultural identity, perception and social values are completely different from Mizos.

But the Mizos were coercive in character, confounded the Reangs towards their (Mizos) path of believe. It was extremely difficult to change the mindset of Reangs, the religiously persuasion was an instinctive dislike among the Reang tribals, which were practiced many years together. The education and health care services provided by Mizo- Christian missionaries had a very adverse impact on Reang society in varying ways of changing their faith, customs, habit and way of living and thinking.

Reang aspirants, through political supporting, came to beckon their own society and people, to re-define their cultural root, searching a social identity, and trying to reconstruct their almost vanishing Reang identity and history.

Demand for Seperate Identity

The process of recognising a separate identity began with their language and culture. That couldn't flourish because of the active dominance of the majority groups within the recognised territorial space in Mizoram, Tripura and Assam. Reangs had a feeling that without strong political support and without having political representation, it was difficult to recognise and upgrade a society.

They started involving ambitious educated Reangs to work together against Mizo domination and discrimination. Realising the necessity of a strong Reang group who can address the Reang situation and establish a position in state politics was its first step. The "revolt process" started with the formation of an apolitical organisation – Reang Peoples Union (RPU), formed in September, 1989.

The main three young aspirants- Sawibunga, the first Reang graduate from North-Eastern Hill University (NEHU) who worked as Head-Master at Lunglei, Laninthanga, a B.Sc student and Ramawia - a primary teacher made their first mark to start the Reang Peoples Union, started from Tuipuibari in Mizoram.

Real action started with the submitting of a memorandum to the Mizoram state government demanding major three issues:

(1) Inclusion of Reang programs in All India Radio, Aizawl,

(2) Reservation of jobs for Reangs in government services and

(3) Nomination of a Reang leader in the legislative assembly.

In fact, when Mizoram became union territory, two Reang leaders Zoduha and Lalnunzira, were nominated as legislators. Subsequently, they (re-Christened as Socio-Cultural Association in December, 1989) also raised other demands such as inclusion of "BRU" in the list of minority tribals, free education up to high school level etc.

Reang Political Organisation

Just a year later, BSCA floated its first political platform, Reang Democratic Convention (RDC), started operating in June 1990, Sawibunga, Chawngzika and Ashiba as its President, Vice-President and General Secretary respectively. The main objective behind to start RDC was for the preservation of Bru culture, customs, language and enriching their socio-economic structure in Mizoram.

Even unifying all Reangs in other states, RDC leaders started interacting with Reangs and sub-clans. The main intention was to bring all Reangs under a common ethnic nomenclature, Bru (named after their ancestor Bruha). The process followed by participating in state elections. In 1992, two Reang leaders Chandra Mohan and Maturi contested district council election in Lai Autonomous District Council (Chhimtuipui district); Chandra Mohan was elected, while Maturai was defeated.

However, the consensus among the insidious Reang forces had reached to a decisive stage. Soaring of Reang trouble and basic rights had started kicking up a great controversy, reaching at the height of major political de-facto in Mizoram.

The development in political domain has a little chance to pace up. Instead that kicked up the whole Mizo-Reang controversy. When Reang contesters failed to secure any representation in the district and assembly elections that further infuriated Reangs to take the path of democratic struggle. The demands rose by Reangs had the genuine supports of few Mizo political parties. Moment the Reang leaders failed to represent in the district and assembly election, the ruling government decided not to further propel the demand of a separate autonomous district council for the Reangs. They shriveled through a united demand and finally spurned off without any support from the government of Mizoram.

Before the Assembly elections, held in November 1993, Reangs were thinking that they would have an easy triumph in getting a separate district council with the support of Chakmas. Politically they merged with the Chakmas's state unit of Bharatiya Janata Party (BJP). The BJP filled eight candidates – three Chakmas and five Reangs, but all were defeated. This pro-Hindu nationalist party, had a strong support to their demands, a section of political cadres and leaders in Mizoram raised the issue for granting the demands of the two political alliance partner Chakmas and the Reangs. That sometime compelled the Mizo leaders to think negatively. The demands raised by Chakmas and Reangs could wane their political powers, and which might also pose a threat to Mizo society.

Demand of Autonomous Council

Any minority tribal group in Mizoram, if talk about autonomy and creation of separate District Council for themselves, what Mizos consider it an attempt to fragment the Mizo State. To them, it is an emotive issue. Deeply thought by the Mizos to counter such demands of minority tribal groups thereby cleverly branded them outsiders who have settled in Mizoram.[4]

The demand of autonomy waged by the Chakma and Reang, what Mizos continuously defended, backed by Mizo political leaders. Mizos Zirlai Pawl (MZP), Mizo National Front (MNF) and Sailo's People Conference (SPC) branded Chakmas as "foreigners from Bangladesh" and the Reangs as "outsiders" from Tripura and Assam. To test their political mettle, these organisations started campaigning vigorously against both the Chakma 'infiltrators' and Reang 'migrants', through village census and quit notices amidst allegations of intimidation and arson in the Chakma and Reang inhabited areas of Mizoram. With slogans such as "*Pathian mik pek Mizoram hi hnam dang hnena pek tun tu chu Mizo te hmelma lian berani*"(Anyone who wants to give this God given Mizoram to non-Mizos is the biggest enemy of us, Mizos).

Situation worsens further instead of fulfilling the demand of separate autonomous district. Reang political leaders became the ally partner of BJP during 1993 assembly elections in Mizoram. They further carried the onerous task of fulfilling the demand through a fresh approach.

On December 1994, Sawibunga founded Bru National Union (BNU), abdicated all political ties, realizing that political tie up would not going to buttress Reang demands, decided to take the neutral path of addressing the Reang demands and other rising problems, started uniting the Reang society after formation of the Reang militant group.

Anti-Reang Campaign

Mizos stepped up to an immediate issue of defranchising Reangs, alleging large-scale deletion of names from the state voter's list. In their pre-planned ostracism of rejecting many Reangs from the voter's list, Mizo organisations were successful, with the support of local authorities, in evicting the Reangs from many villages in Mizoram by leveling them "foreigners" – stirring the anti-foreigners agitation (1995). This had made the Reangs feeling giddy in various threatening situation, allowing them to migrate to the bigger settlement in the proposed RADC areas. In that Mizo political hara-kiri and growing acrimony in Mizoram, Reangs of smaller groups sparsely populated areas of south-west Mizoram, crawled into larger group to save their family and life. But the whole credit of uniting the Reangs in Mizoram went to BNU for the efforts they waged.

The anti-Reang campaign hadn't yet stopped there; they were suffering in another political debacle, when the Mizoram government declared the Dampa forest areas, inhabited by Reangs, as Tiger Wildlife Sanctuary. Government served eviction notices to the Reang families, wildlife project badly affected the thousands of Reang families in the villages of Tuipuibari, Dampa Rengpui, New Chika, Mualvawm, Saipui, Sidon, Lampachera and Persang. Government denied compensating to the victims of the Reang villagers.

Wrong Steps of Government

The sanctuary is recently proposed to be extended to upto Lunglei district covering the villages of Tlabung Dinthar, Hnakkai, Zuanzawl etc. The areas mostly inhabited by Reang families. Knowing the fact, government intention seems biased to alienate the Reangs further, and which would ultimately force the Reangs to flee to different areas from Mizoram, claimed Reang leaders.

That was a wrong step that Mizoram government decided over this 'project making', provoked a section of Bru (Reang) youths to taken up arms, which was reinforced later so-called Bru National Army (BNA) allegedly gunned down a Mizo forest officer Lalzawmliana near Persang village. The incident abated the Mizo youths in communal fare up and later a section of the Mizos fully joined in communal brinkmanship, resulted in burning and destruction of Reang settlements at Tuipuibari, followed by similar incidences in many Reang villages in Mizoram, forced thousands of Reang families fleeing to adjoining areas in Tripura and Assam.

Government of Tripura reported earlier that due to ethnic disharmony and persecution by the Mizos, Reang Refugees of Mamit and Lunglei District of Mizoram had to leave their places. Those families started arriving in Kanchanpur Sub-Division of North District in search of safer shelter, since 29-10-1997. Displaced Reang refugee leaders have also submitted a memorandum to the Government of India on 13-7-1998, stating their grievances and demands. The issue of the Reang migration is sensitive one and multi pronged. The district administration of north Tripura is, however, looking this matter more seriously.[4]

The government figure, however, varies from its genuineness; over 35 thousand Reangs crossed borders and sheltered in Assam and Tripura, the figure which later spilled over up to 52 thousand. " Mizoram human rights groups estimated that some 41,000 Reangs, a tribal group from Mizoram that has been displaced due to the sectarian conflicts, presently sheltered in six refugee camps in north Tripura."[5]

Facts from South Asia Human Rights Documentation Centre (SAHRDC)

"The exodus of Reangs to the adjoining Cachar in Assam and north Tripura started in October 1997 following generalized violence against their community. The controversy started when the Bru National Union, a political party of Reangs formed in the early 90s, in a general assembly meeting in September 1997 passed a resolution demanding Autonomous District Council for the Reangs within Mizoram. There was a strong reaction from Mizo Student Federation (MZP) who said that "if the Reangs wanted to divide or disintegrate Mizoram further, it would be better that they go away. The resolution demanding Autonomous District Council could not be accepted by MZP. If the Reangs go ahead with their plan, the MZP was ready to fight against such a demand. Mizoram is the only land Mizos have and it could not be lost to foreigners or other communities." The Reangs who crossed over to Tripura spoke of "a fear psychosis following the killing in October, 1997 of 10 Reangs, allegedly by the MZP. The flow was not stopped, suggesting tension and lack of security. MZP went on the rampage after the murder of a Mizo forest warden allegedly by the Bru National Liberation Front.

An armed militant group called the Bru National Army (BNA), believed to be the Militant Wing of the Bru National Union (BNU), was formed in 1994 to protect, develop and uplift the Reangs. According to the Bru leaders, their cultural practices were obstructed and they were forced to adopt Mizo names and Mizo languages as their medium of instruction instead of the native Kokbarak. The Bru leaders also alleged that the names of about 20,000 Reangs were deleted from the Electoral Rolls.

The Mizos have always lived in isolation and they have a very strong attachment to their homeland. Thus the moment any minority tribal groups talks of autonomy and demands creation of separate District Council for themselves. Mizos consider it as an attempt to fragment the Mizo State further and it becomes a very emotive issue. To counter such demands such minority tribal groups are branded as outsiders who have settled in Mizoram. And all sorts of attempts are made for de-legitimising their claims by deletion of names from the voters' list, questioning the census report, etc. Any minor incident can provoke a violent reaction from the majority tribal group. In the case of Reangs, killing of a forest warden allegedly by Bru National Army resulted in burning of hundreds of houses of Reangs in many villages and killings of many Reangs. The entire Reang community was considered as the enemy of the Mizo people. Consequently, panic gripped the Reang community and many of them were forced to flee their homes. The insurgent groups affiliated to the minority tribal groups take full advantage of such a situation and project that it is they who can protect the interest of the minority tribal groups. The Bru National Army, the insurgent outfit of the Reangs claims to protect the interests of the Reangs. The Reangs in the adjoining State of Tripura are the second largest tribal community in the State. The internally displaced Reangs from Mizoram took shelter in Tripura with the hope that they would get support from the Reang community of Tripura. Before proposing a possible course of solution, it is proposed to consider U.N. Guidelines on Internal Displacement in the context of internally displaced Reangs. Though any country has not adopted the guidelines, they may help the Reangs to make their demands to the State and the Central Governments. Moreover, these guidelines would make the State and the Central Governments aware of their responsibilities."[6]

"In Mizoram fearing persecution from the ethnic majority Mizos, 15,000 to 50,000 Reang tribals have fled their homes since 1997 and found shelter in north Tripura, border villages of Assam and the Chittagong Hill Tracts of Bangladesh. In order to accelerate the repatriation process, the Tripura government discontinued food rations and medical services in some camps, causing at least 16 people to starve to death. At least 260 IDPs died as a result of inadequate shelter and unclean water, and around 1,400 reportedly became seriously ill. Additionally, displacement camps are susceptible to attacks and mismanagement, for which the National Human Rights Commission castigated the Mizoram government in a 1998 report." [7]

NOTES

1. K.S. Singh (Ed.), *People of India, Mizoram*, Vol 34.
2. Food scarcity in Kanchanpur, 42 thousand Reangs in real trouble, *Dainik Jugasankha*, Guwahati, Assam. March 5, 2000.
3. S.K. Bhattacherjee, *Reang People of India*, Seagull Book, Calcutta, 1995.
4. http://northtripura.nic.in/reang.htm
5. U.S. Department of State (U.S. DOS,Section 2 d), February 2001, 2000 Country Reports on Human Rights Practices [Internet]
6. K.C. Saha, 2000, UN Guiding Principles on Internal Displacements: A Case Study of Internally Displaced Reangs of Mizoram in North-Estern India. [Views expressed in this paper are the author's personal and not of the Government of India].
7. South Asia Human Rights Documentation Centre (SAHRDC), 16 March 2001, No Refuge: the Plight of Conflict-Induced Internally Displaced Persons in India, [Internet].

4 Reangs' Problem after Migration from Mizoram

The relationship between the Reangs and the Mizos virtually came to deadlock in 1996 Lok Sabha Polls when the Mizo National Front (MNF) thronged before Aizawl district election officer, claiming to disenfranchise a large number of Reang tribal voters. The Reangs, on the other hand, revolted against Mizos to disallow their claim of restricting Reangs from their franchise rights. This had dispelled Reangs to settle in different areas of Assam and Tripura.

Around more than 35 thousand Reangs, (35,000 reported by a monthly mazagine *Eastern Panoroma*, in Assam) initially migrated to different areas of Assam and Tripura. Among them eight thousand were languishing in extreme poverty since October 1997, in the make shift temporary settlements in forest areas of Riflemara, Kanchinalla, Ramnathpur, Kalapahar, Bagcherra, Baruncherra, Chaulkhauri near Hailakandi district of Assam and Mizoram Border. In that grave situation Mizoram and Tripura government have not rehabilitated them in time.

Heavy downpour, which often lashed the Barak Valley during monsoon, threw the Reang refugees' usual life out of gear, as their bamboo made huts were flattened by high velocity wind. They had no buffer stock and no land for cultivation at the places where Reangs shaltered that forced them to eat tree leafs and wild animals.

Around ten thousands settled down in various parts of Hailakandi district at Assam and Mizoram bordering areas, suffered in various ill fated diseases, sometime claiming their lives. In absent of adequate food and shelter, many died during their initial arrival at Hailakandi district of Assam. Neither Assam government nor local district administration did come forward, for helping and providing them basic amenities and shelter, during the period of migration. With the initiative of local political leaders the disastrous situation of the Reang refugees brought to the notices of the local administration. On 24 November,1998 Kalyan Ashram along with few doctors of Red Cross and Cancer Hospital of Silchar had first reportedly reached to the Reang refugee camps, in Hailakandi district of Assam, at where Reang refugees took shelter.

Reangs, bashed by Mizos, had also taken shelter in the areas of Gopinathpur, Guaura, Chota Bhubir Bandh and Manapi village of Karimganj district in Assam. Initially they were supported by Karimganj Tribals Union (KTU) and All Assam Mangolayad People's Cultural Organisation (ASMPCO). But getting their rehabilitation, food and shelter were a distant dream to Reang refugees in those unknown areas.[1]

Support of Voluntary Organisations

The two voluntary organisations did their commendable jobs, rehabilitating Reang refugees, distributing 300 sheets of heavy-duty polythene, 10,000 woolen garments for children, 1500 blankets and 1,000 dhotis. Another organisation, Ramkrishna Mission deployed their doctors for saving their lives, supplying life saving drugs and other basic medical facilities apart from supplying clothes, foods and blankets. Without the help of those voluntary organisations, Reang refugees might have been turned at the end of their lives.

Sharing their experience at Reang refugee camps, Tipu Reang said, "We suffered a lot during the monsoon. During rainy seasons we had no food, no shelter and inadequate amount of clothes made us shiver in the cold breeze. State governments, including district administration didn't help us properly. We, however, survived by the help of volunteer organisations like Ramkrishna Mission and Banabashi Kalyan Ashram."[2]

A spokesman of Bru-National Union addressing the media once said that many victims of Reang refugees had managed to escape from the violence-trap in Mizoram, crossed the international border and took shelter in Chittagong Hill Tracts in Bangladesh and away to Myanmar. Around 30 thousand of these Reangs took shelter in Tripura and the population reached upto 40 thousand in Reang refugee camps in Tripura.

The then Tripura revenue minister admitted that hundreds of Reangs died in malnutrition and diseases. According to government report, published by Dainik Jugasankha on 3rd July, 2001 claimed, the death toll reached 1817 numbers in Kanchanpur refugee camps of Tripura. But the non-government sources claimed the number deaths crossed more than 2000 till that date. The deaths occurred only due to the intake of unclean drinking water, many suffered in health diseases and without health treatments.

The situation in the refugee camps of Tripura was intensified and the sufferings of the Reangs ameliorated through initial helps of supplying relief materials to the Reangs by Rastriya Swayamsevak Sangh (RSS) and Kalyan Ashram in addition to relief supplied by Tripura government. But organisations accused the Mizoram government not treating the issue seriously and blamed the government for subverting the Reangs' sombre condition of becoming permanent refugees.

Responses from NHRC and Central Government

with the support of Kalyan Ashram, Reang leaders brought this issue to the notices of the Central Government and National Human Rights Commission to enable their basic rights. Bru leaders and Bru Refugee Committee had to take hard course, starting from meeting the NHRC Chairman Mr. Justice N. Venkatchalaiah, former President Mr. K. R. Narayanan and the then Home Minister L. K. Advani. They sought adequate compensation for the ill affected Reang families during 1998 at Delhi.

NHRC delegates visited twice to these camps to access the situation of Reang refugees. It had served notices to the Mizoram and Tripura governments to take up early measures on Reang issue. But, the intervention of NHRC finally helped the Reang refugees to receive relief funds and cash dole from Central government on regular basis. In October 1999, the delegates of National Human Rights Commission visited Tripura in lieu of solving the most pressing Reang refugee problem, and on 11 October, 1999 Additional Secretary of central government, Chief Secretary of Assam and Tripura jointly attended a discussion in Tripura, but finally failed to gear up that grave situation.[3]

Reang population, during March, 2000, increased at 42,000 in refugee camps at Kanchanpur sub-division of Tripura. The situation was out of administrative control. Government was unable to supply pure drinking water and adequate foods. There were reports of insufficient medicine and doctor services, which resulted huge number of deaths of the Reang refugees in different camps in Tripura. Refugees were unable to receive adequate relief, cash dole, which were provided by government, reportedly irregular. Primary education, which was compulsory to every citizen, a basic right, but it was out of their dream and they were deprived.

In six different refugee camps, non-government organisations had opened primary schools for their education, were on the verge of closure for irregular grants and which they ran without school teacher and infrastructure.[4] Six years after even government did not initiate for opening any single school there. This is another most pathetic story apart from others. They were completely out of school education since last six years.

Allegations Against Relief Distribution

There had been allegations against relief distribution officers for not maintaining timely distribution in several occasions, as the refugees didn't receive regular distribution, reported Bru Refugee Committee's General Secretary- Lalduwang Liayana and Joint Secretary Chandramani Malosi. Without any genuine reason and survey, a local government officer, who was the in-charge of relief distribution, obliterated 10,971 Reang refugees' name from the refugee list.[5] It had further inflicted the problem in refugee camps and many deprived from food and other governmental, benefits. Against this unfair practice, BRC took stern steps, sat for stir, attended rallies and urged the government to punish the officer.

A government report revealed, the numbers of cardholder Reang families in Kanchanpur Sub-division were 6156 up to June 2000 and the total population estimated were 33,361. The families with cardholders were 290. During 1997 – 2000, the childbirth was 1595 and 1670 died in various diseases. The death rate recorded highest in there refugee camps. The numbers of people above 8 years were 26,112 and below 8 years were recorded only 5,553.[6] Just after few days, a report released by relief and rehabilitation minister of Tripura revealed the different figures of the number of Refugees were actually 39,263 in Kanchanpur sub-division. The relief grants received by Tripura government from Centre up to July 19,2000 shot up Rs.22, 25,44,000 and it invested Rs.18, 28,33,574.[7]

According to Kanchanpur Sub-division S.D.O report, on 29.10.97 the total population of Reang refugees was 6,856 and it reached at 10,092 on 9.11.97.During January 1999: it recorded the highest number of refugees which stood at 37,020. Among them 2020 were the new comers. Around 83 percent of the total population was recorded adults. But the population came down at 31,206 as on 20.2.2002.

The distribution of ration was taking place fortnightly basis of 450 gm. of rice per adult per day and 225 gm. per minor per day and 15 gm. salt per head per day and 7.50 gm. per head per day for minor. Besides that the payment of cash dole was made Rs.2.67 per day per adult and Rs.1.33 per day per minor and Rs.20 is made to each family for purchasing of coconut oil. This all mentioned in the government notification No.F.2(a) RR/REANG/98/1 dated 20.7.98 issued by the director, relief and rehabilitation, Government of India. It had also directed to issue *musur dal* 50 gm per day, edible oil 5 gm, dry fish Rs. 30 per day, dry chilly Rs.22, fire-wood Rs. 40 for each adult or to distribute the equivalent amount as mentioned and directed by government of India.[8]

Death Traps in Refugee Camps

In fact, the pernicious problem of drinking water had badly affected the lives of many Reang refugees. It had claimed more than two thousand lives in the refugee camps and most of them become sick in poor health. Only in diarrhea, it claimed around 300 lives, in a single year (*Dainik Jugasankha*, June 1999). It clearly indicates the negligence of local government and health department for providing impure drinking water.

The Assam Tribune reported, "Death stalks Reang refugees now sheltered in six camps in Kanchanpur sub-division in north Tripura district. The Reangs or Brus (now about 32,000 in total), who fled from neighbouring Mizoram following fierce ethnic clashes with Mizos in October-November 1997, are now a miserable lot. Uncertainty looms large over their future as several rounds of talks for their repatriation in Mizoram failed to yield any result. The Reang camps have become virtually death traps as diseases and malnutrition take their toll every year during this time".[4]

According to Tuichharai Bru, president of Mizoram Bru Refugee Committee, while 25 inmates, mainly children and old persons died in malaria during the last 10 days, the figure stood at 250 in the last one year. He alleged that the civil and health administration failed to provide adequate medical facilities to the refugees. As the report of deaths poured in from the camps, the administration sent medical teams to the affected areas. The shortage of medicines as well as health staff has made their task impossible. The two doctors, during 2002, were present in the camps couldn't cope with the fast deteriorating situation. Dr Shiromani Debbarma maintained that they could not arrest the occurrence of deaths for dearth of medicines.

The inmates alleged that the civil administration did not take necessary steps for providing safe drinking water. For example, at Kashirampara refugee camp, out of five ring-wells, four are dried up while out of 13 mark-II tube-wells, nine are out of order."[9]

However, it has been admitted by the local administration to this author that the administration was facing difficulties providing pure water at refugee camps. They said, refugees living far-flung areas from this administrative office, which was out of their capacity to provide supply water. They, however, claimed for installation of RCC wells and mark-II tube wells in all six different camps. In their official report mentioned of 15 mark-II tube-wells and 16 RCC wells installed, have been catering the needs of around 40 thousand Reang refugees' drinking water, which means, a tube-well or a well was shared by 1290 persons.

Basic Amenities

Another problem in the camps is that most of installed tube wells are non-functional, which are not even repaired after installation. But the refugees have been accused, they are responsible for this problem and they are largely unaware how to handle the tube wells. The sanitary latrines constructed in different camps are also inadequate in accordance to such big population of refugees.

During 1998-99, around 951 numbers of sanitary latrines were constructed in those camps, according to a Tripura government report. But many of the Reang refugees have been seen to use plain ground. That damaged the hygiene environment at the camps. NHRC during their visit sought for construction of more sanitary latrines. Local administration claimed they are in construction of more latrines in the camps.

The initial years in the camps were a very panic one. Feeding all the people and sheltering them was a very difficult task before Tripura government. "The local administration was busy round the clock in house listing and finding actual number of refugees. Sometime the list made by the government after census, expressed resentments and deep anger by the Reang refugee leaders. There was always a conflict in-between government and refugee leaders. They never agreed upon the list made by Tripura administration. Local administration made their best to get a correct list of refugees, which was acceptable to both the government and Reang leaders."

Problem in Relief Distribution

Then the trouble came on relief distribution. With those little grants that hardly satisfied all hungry people. Government was providing 450 gm of rice and Rs.2.50 cash dole per day. But refugee leaders claimed, this government supply is insufficient and repeatedly asked to increase the quantity upto 500 gm of rice and Rs. 4.50 per day." said Uttam Kumar Chakma, former SDO, Kanchanpur Sub-division, Tripura, "Government has many limitations and presently only one doctor deployed, who visits all six camps once in a week. In case of any emergency, they have no option for quick medical checkup and treatment, within 10 km ranges they will not find any doctor, but will have to wait for the government doctor. Over last six years of their existence in refugee camps, government has not initiated for their education. It was Kalyan Ashram who arranged refugee children' education in camps."

Simultaneously, local administration has been suffering many uneventualities, fortnightly distribution of rice in one hand and the distribution of cash dole on the other hand. In both cases, S.D.O has to visit camps along with all official staff. "Most of the time we keep ourselves busy in the affairs of several relief distribution. SDO office has very little time left for administrative functioning. There was the need of handling this relief works by a specialist group, than us. Staff were very less, with one UDC, two block In-charge, and three group D staff, which were very less to handle the responsibility," said Chakma.

"With the settlement of Reang Refugees in Kanchanpur sub-division of Tripura, it badly affected the demography of local population. The incidents of communal clashes have been taking place regularly; many innocent local inhabitants fell in victims and many of them suffered for further trafficking to other areas. This has given extra burden to government, and for their shelter, again, local government had to build different camps. This ethnic problem increased during 2000 in the sub-division.

In those ethnic disturbances, various organisations have alleged that the Reang migrants were creating communal disturbances and actively involved in cattle and other goods lifting. They encroached the land of local non-tribals for meeting their daily needs and livelihood. That compelled the non-tribal villagers of Kashirampur to migrate and shelter at Dasda temporary relief camp.

Another constant problem was the degradation of environment and ecological imbalances. Initially they took shelter in deep forest of Kanchanpur sub-division of north Tripura. The places where they were rehabilitated which now has taken the shape of a desert land. The camps are situated at semi-hilly areas, 2 km away from Mizoram-Tripura border.

The refugees have destroyed most of the forest resources and used them for the construction of their houses. The forest is used for meeting their daily firewood consumption. It is estimated that the requirement for their daily consumption is around 55,000 kg fire-wood. Most of the fire-wood are collected within the locality of 5 sq km, and such practice of daily collection of fire-wood is destroying tall and big trees of that locality.

To prevent the unhealthy practice of communal violence and environment degradation, local administration chalked few buffer solutions out, established a local committee to monitor the problem. In case of communal clashes at any individual or community level, committee will oust out the immediate solution. Refugees were asked to stay inside the camps. But this hardly changed the situation, due to poor monitoring and vigilance. As a result, Reangs have been capturing many vacant forest lands for their cultivation and attending deforestation.

"The initial years were most pathetic and traumatic. Those who sheltered in Tripura, were screaming for food, shelter and security. They had to struggle almost every day for food and ate whatever available in the forest, starting from the tree leaf to all sorts of living animals.

Their overt grief can't be expressed in words without observation. I have seen them closely. But no one stood behind to extend the help except Kalyan Ashram. Kalyan Ashram provided two doctors apart from all basic amenities, foods, dresses, winter blankets and medicine for two years. Schools were established for their education and 28 meritorious students were sent outside the state of Tripura, for their higher education. Their whole expenditures were borne out by Kalyan Ashram and around 700 Reang students, in refugee camps, have received primary education through the schools ran by Kalyan Ashram" opined Harihar Prasad, Asst. Organisation Secretary, Kalyan Ashram, Kanchanpur.

Conflict on Social Services

He, however, agreed that with the intervention of NHRC, refugees have started getting all facilities from central government, but charged for rampant corruption prevailing in relief distribution. Around fifty percent of the grants were siphoned out by political leaders and government officials. "We were not taken for any relief distribution.The government supply is insufficient and inadequate that sometime provokes the tension in relief camps. There was a strong allegation of scrapping and pumping out of relief funds, food and medicine. These were taken basically for distribution in refugee camps".[10]

It was observed that Reang refugee conflict has taken a shape of religious conflict. Christian missionary wanted that they should provide all services to the Reang refugees and Hindu missionary should not be there for any help. As a result of this conflict a doctor was brutally killed, who was deployed for refugees' health services. Now they have withdrawn all services and doctor services were terminated.

Lalduhawma Chorkhy, Joint Secretary and Publicity In-charge of Bru Refugee Committee (BRC) said the situation in the camps worsen further when government stopped providing doctors. Private doctors are hardly available in such remote locality like ours. It has been approached to local authority but that does not make any sense to listen our problem. This is one thrust area in which refugees are mostly suffered, died and still suffering.

The other problems are: insufficient distribution pattern of government relief, the cash dole what refugees receive after three months (e.g. during March-April, 2002), the quantity of rice supply is very less from the actual government allocation, the problem of electricity and scarcity of water. Government didn't supply any electricity in refugee camps and few tube wells installed were unable to meet the demand of such big population.

Government has not provided any funds for education, since the very coming of these camps. It was only through the initiative of Kalyan Ashram a school was opened. Few educated Reangs voluntarily involved in community education even without any remuneration. Thousands of Reang children are pouring into backwardness in absence of any education. It is one of the prime concerns of Reang society. Without any government attention and help that can't be solved. There is no formal or informal education facility in refugee camps. Complained Reang refugees.

Literacy rate is very low or almost negligible. There are only three graduates and one master's degree-holder. "We are trying to call up few more Reang graduates from Mizoram to take up the education program for refugee children. The sadest part of our life is that being the citizens of this country we are deprived of all our fundamental rights. We are supposed to get all facilities as like other citizens are enjoying and we are simply living as refugees" said a refugee leader.

Even in Mizoram, Reangs have no equal rights and lagging far behind the others. They are all waiting for a normal life, as the early repatriation is highly required. They would like to go back to Their homeland—Mizoram, as early as possible. The present situation has turned more critical, now they cann't return without the help of Mizoram government.

Sri Krishna Raghunath Vhide, Organisational Secretary of Kalyan Ashram in Tripura said that initially local Reang villagers provided their land and forest to the migrant Reangs for temporary shelter. Kalyan Ashram gave them all moral support and supplied all basic materials through voluntarily collection from various places. The situation is taking a serious turn now; refugee people are becoming lazy, mentally and physically weak. Their health conditions are deteriorating regularly.

Although, central government recognised Reangs as refugees. They are getting nominal cash dole and insufficient quantity rice. For inadequate security in the camps Kalyan Ashram had to stop medical facility. The refugee leaders were not sure about the safety of the medical personnel.

Initially they have suffered for many unwanted reasons." I have seen their sufferings, when they first came to this place losing almost everything in the riots perpetuated in Mizoram. There was a great fear rallied around them because, many of them had to lose some of their relatives in the attacks set out by Mizos in Mizoram. They were looking happy when they have started gathering help from NGOs and government agency. They had gained their optimism when they realized that NHRC and Courts are there to provide them the legal justice. They further lost their hopes in returning their homeland and when they observed that Mizoram government has not obeyed the Court and NHRC. This is really an unfortunate story that can happen to any human society," Vhide said.

He further informed that there will be more than 25 thousand Reangs till living in Mizoram, who are not free from atrocities and community violence. They are unable to exercise their fundamental rights. In Mizo society, they are not recognised as Reangs due to loss of their traditional customs, culture and language and they are bound to follow the Mizo culture. They are backward and poor in wealth.

A survey was conducted at refugee camps revealed many interesting facts of their perception and choices. Around 69 percent of the refugee population have sorted out the repatriation is their major problem, while 23 percentage believe the education, 15 percent believe poverty and 7.6 percent believe employment is their big problem. Among them cent per cent believe the lack of infrastructure and education facility provided in the refugee camps and the same per cent of the population also realize the insufficient food and medicine supply. In the survey, it has identified around 38.46 per cent of the refugee population use raw water, 46.15 per cent use deep tube wells and rest 15.38 per cent use pond and other sources of raw water. While 76 per cent of the refugee population have no sanitary facility and 24 per cent of them can avail only that facility. 92 per cent respondents representing the population of the refugee camps said they were affected by communal violence. Due to continious communal violence and torture they had to leave Mizoram and remaining of the population left the state for less government attention, and 92.30 per cent of the refugee population expressed their unwillingness to return Mizoram believing the fact that their lives will be in danger again. As many as 90 per cent blamed Mizoram government responsible for their unholy situation and only 7 per cent blamed central government for not solving this dispute. Around 76.92 per cent still feel they are not safe in refugee camps and 15.38 per cent said there is further the chance of communal violence. Regarding the most pressing refugee problem, 61 per cent of them still uncertain about their future and 30.76 per cent believe the entire solution is now with government.

NOTES

1. Uttam Kumar Shee and Mithulala Choudhuury, "Many Reangs trace of without children", *Dainik Sonar Cachar*, December, 1998. Silchar, Assam.
2. Surajit Thakur, "Living on the edge, Reang refugees in Limbo", *Eastern Panorama*, June, 1998, Guwahati.

3. *Dainik Jugasankha*, July 20, 2000.
4. Food scarcity in Kanchanpur, 42 thousand Reangs in real trouble, *Dainik Jugananakha*, March 5, 2000, Guwahati & Silchar.
5. Thousand Reang Refugees in absence of Food. *Dainik Jugasankha*, June, 1999.
6. 1670 persons died in Refugee camps within three years. *Dainik Jugasankha*, 16 July 2000. Guwahati .
7. Rs. 22 crore granted for Reang refugees, *Dainik Jugasankha*, 20 July, 2002.
8. U.K.Chakma, Sub Divisional Officer, Kanchanpur, North Tripura, Government of Tripura.
9. "Reang refugees in Tripura camps a miserable lot" *The Assam Tribune*, 17 June 2001, [Internet].
10. Diarrhea, malaria in Reang camps, 1817 died, *Dainik Jugasankha*, July 3, 2001.Guwahati.

5 Killing and Torture of Reangs: A Violation of Human Rights

Before 1989, there was no violence and ethnic clash between Mizos and Reangs in Mizoram. The entire problem surfaced after 1989, when Reangs postulated to recognise their culture, identity and language. That volatile situation took a different shape after 1993 Assembly election, wherein all Reang candidates, who aspired to make their political representation in Assembly, were defeated. Moment the state government was formed, it dismissed their plea for autonomous council. Mizo organisations such as MZP, MNF and SPC became the surmountable barriers in the path of Reangs' democratic movement. A strong campaign was launched by these organisations against Reangs and Chakmas of Mizoram, leveling Chakmas as "foreigners" and Reangs as "outsiders". Chakmas somehow managed to survive in Mizoram for their huge population.

The trivial point of Reang controversy boiled up from there and Reangs were severally threatened by Mizo society. To dismantle their democratic movement, which followed by influencing the whole section of the Mizo society in Mizoram, many Reang voters were short-listed and pruned the names illegally by the systematic approach with strong political support.

In the second phase, eviction notices were served forcefully to push the Reangs out of Mizoram. Denying to carry eviction orders, which sometime forced the Reangs to face the reign of terror.

Between the period of 1994-1997, it had claimed many lives, Reang villages were torched, girls were raped, and all the minimum grants and facilities were stopped. In spite of taking any action, Mizoram government was completely in the spiral of silence, government police was inactive and unwilling to take any action, entirely guided by Mizo organisations and backed by indirect support of Mizo leaders.

During the 1999 Lok Sabha election in Mizoram many Reangs could not exercise their franchise rights. The Mizoram goverment, during the election, 1999, after a direction of Delhi High Court, had set two polling stations at the Mizoram-Tripura bordering areas to enable the Reang refugees to cast their votes. State government claimed to made adequate security and transport arrangements for the Reang refugees to enable them to exercise their franchise in Mizoram.

The then district magistrate had averred that more than 31,000 Reang refugees were in the relief camps, but only 1198 of them were included in the Mizoram voters' list. On the other hand the refugee leaders had been claiming that the number of voters would be over 18,000. The Mizoram government had intentionally deleted the names of a large number of Reang voters from the electoral list, the Reang leaders alleged.

Raping of Reang Girls and Killing Reang People

According to Mizoram Chief Electoral Officer, the Reang voters were identified on the basis of the electoral rolls prepared on July 21, 1999 by the Mizoram government. Meanwhile, the influential students' body in Mizoram had protested against the setting up of the special polling stations.[1]

The demand of a Reang district council raised by Reangs in Mizoram was absolutely justified and logical, considering the other tribal groups, for instance, Chakmas and Maras having their own councils. But Mizoram government quibbled over the issue, further perplexing their genuine demands.

Instead, Mizoram government issued arrest warrants falsely alleging the Reangs involved in state sponsoring terrorism. Reangs were treated as third class citizen,and they had no right in maintaining their religious prayers and cultural wisdom. They had no right in education, deprived from government jobs and community development.

In anti-Reangs campaign in Mizoram during 1994-97, hundreds of girls belonging to Reang society were ravished, houses torched and many killed. Temples were blazed," averred Bru committee member Kripamohan Reang.[2]

Countering the Mizoram Government's stand, Bru National Convention of India (BNCI) general secretary Bimal Reang said, "Despite the fact that we constitute the second largest ethnic community in Mizoram, we have been denied all constitutional rights and civic amenities over the years." He said that Reangs had taken Mizo names and many of them had converted to Christianity, the dominant religion among Mizos. Tuisarai Bru said, "many of us adopted Mizo culture as well." He added that "our fate remained the same" in spite of doing this.

Protection of Reang Rights

Although Mizoram is India's second most literate state after Kerala, the literacy rate within Reang society is less than one per cent. The Reang community until now has only five graduates in Mizoram. Tuisarai Bru stated: "Against this backdrop, we wanted to free ourselves from the yoke of Mizos and hence raised our voice for constitutional provisions to become civilised citizens." [3] We were treated as second-class citizens here," said Hmangaisha, president of the Mizoram Bru Refugee Committee, Ashapara camp. "While Mizos get free education, health service and food, we have to pay through our nose. Even educated Reangs can't expect a government job. The very word Bru (Reang) is a taboo to the Mizos."[4]

The relationships between Reang and Mizos had pared down when Bru (Reang) National Union (BNU), established in 1994, started fighting for the cause of protection of Reang rights. Subsequently, BNU submitted the demand for creation of autonomous council to Mizoram Chief Minister Lalthanhawla. Since then the relationship between two communities was razed down completely.

Attacking on Reang villages and their lives by Mizos had become norm of the community clashes between two groups. Mizo activists set afire at least 1300 houses of Reang inhabitants in the 41 Reang dominated villages in Mizoram. The Mizo miscreants damaged 365 well-built houses and 30 religious temples.[5]

On July 10,1998 *The Assam Tribune* reported that Mizos served orders to disown their (Reangs) traditional Hindu culture and identity and urged Reangs to convert into Christianity.

The Indian Constitution identified them a separate scheduled tribe entity and according to that provision they should continue to maintain their ethnic identity, deeply regretted by all sections of Indian society for violation of their rights in Mizoram. They had to pay a heavy price being a minority in Mizoram. Mizos, at the behest of Mizo leaders, attacked on several Reang villages.

Apart from burning houses, many Reangs were beaten to death, 45 women were raped in Reang villages of Mizoram following the BNU demand. Fifty one thousand Reangs living in 80 villages of Mizoram were forced to migrate in the bordering areas of Assam, Tripura, Bangladesh and far to Myanmar.

Mizo Miscreants

Mizos, even did not allow the Reangs to live at bordering areas of Mizoram. Mizo miscreants, with the help of Mizo police, have served notices to the Reang inhabitants of Ghutghuti, Rifelmara and Sahebmarra villages in Hailakandi district of Assam and asked them to quit. Around 262 houses of Reangs were burnt down by those Mizo miscreants, who also resorted physical attack on the Reang men and sexually assaulted their women, described in a memorandum submitted to the former Assam Chief Minister Prafulla Kumar Mahanta, by the Evicted Reang Relief Committee (ERRC). It mentioned about two thousand Reangs were critically injured in various inhuman atrocities by a section of Mizos. In that growing acrimonies, Assam state administration did set up two police outposts at Ghutghuti and Jayanpunj on the Assam-Mizoram bordering areas to prevent the attacks on Reangs.

Smt. Ubati Reang, a leading social worker among Reang society, said that her meeting with central government leaders and ministers had not brought any bear-fruit results. Central leaders were not very sympathized to the Reang cause and to take measures and action.[6]

When the situation was in extreme rife, Mizo miscreants demanded that the Reang inhabitants in Assam at bordering areas should also vacate the land. (It is at the disputed lands of two states: Assam and Mizoram.) Series of administrative level meetings were held in this connection, solving the border dispute and to prevent the Mizos from further attacks on Reangs in Assam.

MLA Gautam Roy, presently a minister of Assam state government, complaining to NHRC mentioned that their rights have been violated. The refugees have to be treated properly as they are also human beings. Another NGO, HADSA, headquarters at Hailakandi in Assam, filed complaints to NHRC regarding the violations of human rights of Reang refugees.

Eastern Panorama, a magazine, reported that 25 young girls had been raped by Mizo youths in the relief camps of Assam and many youths of the camps reportedly kidnapped and later untraced. Mizoram police had been suspected for these deeds.

Quit Notices

A preach letter of Mizo Zirlai Pawl (MZP) headquarter in Aizawl, issued by V.Lhluapa, memo no-109/50/97, dated 23,10.1997 published by *Dainik Sonar Cachar*, a regional Bengali daily of Assam, on December, 1998, mentioned about the letter saying that "forgive Mizoram by those non-Mizos are living". The letter was distributed in the entire Mizoram on behalf of MZP chief leader Khauliana, threatening all non-Mizos to quit Mizoram.

Though it was written in Mizo language, but its meaning comes out like this – *Those who receive this letter, if non-mizos are to quit Mizoram shortly and those Mizos if receive this letter are requested to announce this information in their locality. Breaking of this order will be taken with serious punishment.* MZP members openly made this publicly in city and village areas in Mizoram that the Reangs if not leave the state immediately, their property will be captured, they will be killed and the beautiful girls will be raped. In that open mass statement and barbarity, Mizoram government was fragile to take any action. [7]

On October 1997, a media report confirmed that Mizo youths of MZP and other organisations ambushed some poor Reangs in the state and killed some of them and several young girls were abused sexually at Chokarthal and Bethani Jum basti areas of Mizoram. In those discernible attacks, at least sixty percent of Reangs were forced to convert themselves into Christianity.

Cutting and scrapping the Reang voters from voter list during 1996 Lok-sabha polls malafided their franchisee rights and it was believed that it has given the berth of Bru Revolutionary Army (BRA), an outlawed organisation of Reangs, started fighting to regain their rights against the " disenfranchise discrimination."

Oppositely, Mizo people also complained against BRA as Reangs were antisocial and anti-nationals. On 4th March 1998, Mizo youth organisations like MZP, MRP, YMA and MAP jointly toppled attacking Reangs at Gutghuti village of Hailakandi district in Assam, alleged gang raping of some Reang women, torched 172 huts and two schools ran by Banabashi Kalyan Ashram.[8]

In another series of attacks on October 7,1997 many Reangs rendered homeless, sheltered in refugee camps. One such disgraceful man, Manu Reang, by profession a cycle mechanic who used to live in Bairabhi block of northwest Mizoram. Describing his most pitiable incidence said, "It was on 7 October,1997, the Bairabhi block was cocooned in silence that night. In the dead of night, we heard the sound of knocking at the door. I saw a gang of Mizo youths standing outside, when I opened the door. They asked my wife. She was out of station, when I said and immediately beaten up. They said me to go Church and pray to Jesus or pray for my death. But when I refused they set my house in fire."

Communal Tension

In the increasing strife between Reang and Mizos, Mizoram government, however, deployed security forces at Reang populated Dampa areas of West Mizoram, but suddenly withdrew without any reason. Mizo Peoples Conference (MPC), an opposition political party of Mizoram, severally criticized government's decision of lifting the security forces (C.R.P.F.). The MPC expressing their resentment said that the lifting CRPF forces from Reang areas would swell the tension among Reang society.

The Chief Secretary of Mizoram government, however, assured them to re-deploy ' Mizo Armed Force' at Reang areas. The Bru National Armed Force (BNLF), a militant outfits organisation was then fighting for Reang democratic rights, had threatened to the state government to bring the militant action if violence further replicate in Reang areas like 1997.[9]

Onkar Shing Lakhabat, an MP from Rajasthan, once visited to those refugee people along with a group of his party delegates. Baiyanti a married women expressing the trouble-torn situation in Mizoram said to Lakhabat - "I was luckily better than worse, alive otherwise. I would have faced the similar consequences as Sia and Kumbi had faced. Both sia and Kumbi were raped by Mizo youths just one day after their marriage.[10]

The BNLF had launched many terror attacks on Christian community and Mizos. BNLF militants assassinated four Christian missonaries in Mizoram on 25 April, 2000. Victor Crista, the Church father at Kanmune in Mizoram, was brutalty killed. Mizoram government alleged BNLF involvement in that carnage.

According to a PTI report on 24 November, 1998 in which Mizoram government Chief Secretary suspected BNLF could bring attack on the eve of Assembly election held on November, 1998. Those days, the Mizo-Reang conflict, in Mizoram, flanged down the peace and prosperity within all sections of the society and a grim fear was billowing around. The situation was absolutely out of government control. Sometime Mizo organisations had restricted the non-Mizos of free exercise of their rights through imposition of special notices. It had posed threat even to many other communities living in Mizoram. During the month May, 2002 MZP called for a *bandh* for 48 hours in the state.During the bandh it restricted the non-Mizos to attend any business, offices, schools and colleges. They were not allowed to go outside of their houses.[11]

Looting, snatching, and tax collection on regular basis, by the youth students, are the common features of the state. Non-Mizos (not only Reangs) don't have the genealogy to talk about their rights. Most of them have to live by their mercy. Mizoram is the living land of many non-Mizos—Reangs, Ckakmas, Mars and others. All are living in dysfunctional social system. Democracy is a social eclipse, not means the rights of common people.

NOTES

1. *UNI report* / www.newslinks.rediff.com
2. Reangs are unwilling to return if demands are not promised, Dainik Jugasankha, July, 1 2001.
3. Syed Sajjad Ali, "Social Tension: The Reang refugees", *Frontline*, Vol. 15, July 18 - 31, 1998.
4. Tapash Ganguly, Strangers in their motherland, The Week, Oct 24, 1999.
5. Death Galore, *Northeast Sun*, New Delhi – August, 1998.
6. Gastro breaks out in Hailakandi refugee camps, *The Assam Tribune*, July 10, 1998.
7. Uttam kumar Shee & Mithulala Choudhuury, Many Reangs Traces without children, *Dainik Sonar Cachar*, December, 1998 . Silchar, Assam.
8. Surajit Thakur, Living on the edge, Reang refugees in limbo, *Eastern Panorama*, June, 1998. Guwahati.
9. Resentment over lifting forces from Reang areas. *Dainik Jugasankha*, May, 16, 2000.
10. Refugee problem may invite terrorism, *Dainik Jugasankha*, April 8, 1999.
11. Non-Mizos are restricted to go outside, *Dainik Jugasankha*, May 25, 2000.

6 Reang's Democratic Struggle Vs. Terrorism

During Lok Sabha polls in 1996, Mizo National Front (MNF) threatened the Aizawl district election officer to disenfranchise a large number of Reang tribal voters. It was believed that the then election officer pervaded that political influence in election, striving for Mizos integrity, against Reang's rights and interests.

To refrain the political clout in Mizrom, Bru Revolutionary Army (BRA), a militant outfit organisation of Reangs has emerged. They arranged all sophisticated arms supplied from Bangladesh and Myanmar and got rebellion training from National Socialist Council of Nagaland (NSCN, I-M) at the deep forest of the Indo-Myanmar border.

It was learnt that some Reang youths turned violent aftermath of the Mizoram government's decision to declare the Dampa forest areas, inhabited by Reangs, as Tiger Wildlife Sanctuary. It provoked a section of the Bru youth to take up arms, as we know the organisation Bru National Liberation Front (BNLF).

BNLF Militancy

Terrorism, in general, catapulted in Reang society from the general awareness of their basic rights, discrimination on the basis of religion, government's dual policy on programme implementation and dismissing the demand of district autonomous council by the government. BNLF taken up arms and ammunitions when government shown its disinterest and apathy to mitigate Reang demands.

Established in the middle of 1998, BNLF incarnated the demands and pushing continuous pressure on government. Before the establishment of Reang terrorist organisation government put a deaf ear on Reang issue. BNLF militants launched massive attacks on Mizos in several places of the state, in the act of revenging earlier Mizo-offences. That had changes the attitude of the government for having a sort of dialogue with Reang leaders. As a result the bilateral discussions in-between Mizoram government and Bru (Reang) leaders took place, which are now hold regularly.

The efforts of bringing all tribal communities under one umbrella, BNLF started massive campaign in various Reang dominated areas of north Tripura. Though both the outfits were based in Mizoram, they were capable enough to influence both sections of Reang society in Mizoram and Tripura.

After deliberate attempts to mobilize Mizoram government's attention, it has started mobilizing all tribals in Tripura on autonomous agenda. The early move by the Tripura Tribal Areas Autonomous District Council (TTAADC), most influential organisation has the larger role in bringing all tribes together and claiming *Kokborok* their language. This sparked off another controversy in northeast.

Reangs, demanded the reorganization of their community as a separate entity. The second biggest tribal group of Tripura state had demanded recognization of their language the *"Kaubru"* as their official language of the state. At present, *"Bengali"* and *"Kokborak"* languages are recognized as the official languages in Tripura.

Chala Laimchaha Bru, the commander of the BLA in his statement said that the move of the TTAADC was an attempt to subjugate the Reangs by the majority, the Debbarmans. He threatened to launch an armed struggle, if required to get due recognition of Reang language.[1] The BNLF and the BRA attended a secret meeting at Karimganj in Assam, which was aimed to finalise strategies to combat moves by various organisations against the Reangs.

During 2000, Mizoram government moved a strong allegation against BNLF for their activities in Mizoram, that has subdued the return of Reang refugees.

Prime Minister at Delhi called up a meeting on the issue of *Terrorism in Northeast,* attended by all chief ministers of northeast. Mizoram Chief Minister Joramthanga expressed his concern of returning the Reang refugees possible only when BNLF would stop terror attacks. BNLF was involved in killing of four Christian missionaries in Mizoram on 25 April 2000 alleged Mizoram government.[2]

On September 23,1999 suspected BNLF terrorists set off a bomb blast near Zawlpui hamlet in Lunglei district. No one was injured in the attack that was possibly meant to target a moving jeep carrying government personnel proceeding on election duty. On April 19,2000 suspected BNLF terrorists abducted a school teacher near a village along the Mizoram-Tripura border.

BNLF kidnapped six NEPCO workers from Turial Hydel Project on March, 30,2000. That incident mired the government in controversy. The opposition party MPC protested strongly against government move to handle the situation effectively. BNLF threatened the government to deploy security forces at Reang villages. (Security forces were lifted by the government). It has, however, forced the government to decide on the security arrangement in Reang villages in Mizoram.

On June 30,2000 suspected BNLF terrorists killed seven members of the anti-terrorist Hunter Force of Mizoram Police and injuring four others in an ambush along the India-Bangladesh border in Mamit district. On September 3 2000, 14 BNLF terrorists killed in an internecine clash with the NLFT at the latter's Thangnan base camp in the Chittagong Hill Tracts, Bangladesh.

BNLF also killed 10 NLFT terrorists in retaliation. In September 22,2002 two BNLF terrorists were killed in an encounter in the Ratabari block (administrative unit) of Karimganj district, Assam. Surjo Moni and Hmunsiama, the President and 'Deputy Commander' of BNLF taken hostage by NLFT on July 9, 2000 and escaped from their captivity. On November 19, 2000 BNLF's hand suspected in the Borahaldi carnage that claimed 14 lives. BNLF terrorist killed in raid by security forces on its hideout in Bhuban Hills in Cachar district of Assam on August 11,2001.

Aims and Objectives of BNLF

Protection of rights and dignity of the Reangs are the two primary objectives that the outfit has proclaimed. My discussions with various Reang groups clearly exhibit the demands of BNLF and its pattern of function.

Besides its own rights and dignity, BNLF endeavours to protect language and religious identity of Reangs, which it claims to be Hinduism. This is manifested in its vehement opposition to the alleged imposition of Christianity on Reangs. It has also demanded a separate Reang homeland in Mizoram.

Subsequently, it transformed its stand and aimed to achieve a separate ADC, and reservation in the Mizoram Legislative Assembly for the community. Besides, it has also taken up with the Mizoram government the issue of repatriation of Reang refugees who had been displaced during the October 1997 ethnic clashes.

Currently, they are neither demanding for any political position in Mizoram Assembly nor they are demanding for any territorial autonomy as raised by other terrorist organisations in northeast. It has agreed to the demand for an ADC and settle for a regional council. It has compromised to settle all its demands for the greater interest and settlement of Reang refugees, so that the refugees can get an opportunity for peaceful leaving.

Leadership, Area of Operation and Operational Strategy

They have maintained a strong base in creating a terrorist gang through active leadership and were successful to get engage larger populace of the Reang youths to join hands in terrorism, to strive for the goals of Reang autonomy and rights, which were denied in Mizoram. Thang Masha is the current President of the BNLF. The outfit's cadre strength is estimated to be a little over 100. Other important leaders of the outfit include Surjo Moni Reang and Hmunsiama, President and 'Deputy Commander' respectively.

In the year 2000, both had managed to escape from the clutches of National Liberation Front of Tripura (NLFT) terrorists, who were holding them captive, in January 2001 and had subsequently surrendered. They have since been in police custody. Other leaders of the outfit include A Joseph, 'Advisor', Solomon Prophul, 'General Secretary' and S. Bru, the 'Organising Secretary'.

The BNLF suffered its worst reverse when the then 'General Secretary', Hambai Mshoy, and the then 'Army Chief', Sheing Molshoy, were killed in an internecine clash with the NLFT on July 9, 2000, at a camp in Bangladesh.

Areas in which BNLF cadres are active include parts of Mizoram, Tripura and Assam. The areas where the outfit has carried out major attacks include the Mamit and Lunglei districts of Mizoram, the Hailakandi district of Assam and Kanchanpur sub-division of north Tripura district. The BNLF is also known to be operating in the dense forests along the Mizoram-Tripura border. Besides, its hideouts are located in the Bhuban Hills of Cachar district in Assam.

The outfit is involved in selective abduction for ransom, which is a major source of finance for the terrorist group. In this, non-Reangs and Mizo Christians are the primary targets. Besides, the BNLF is also involved in violent attacks not only against non-Reangs, but also against security force personnel. The outfit was also engaged in internecine clashes with other terrorist outfits in the northeast, like the National Liberation Front of Tripura (NLFT).

Furthermore, its cadres carry out attacks with modern weapons like AK series assault rifles, grenades and bombs, and are well trained. The BNLF uses both conventional and guerrilla tactics in its attacks.

Linkages and Networks

It has maintained a strong links and networks not with the Indian terrorist groups but also have lings with some international organisations. Such links have enabled them to procure arms and arrange trainings for the cadres. Among its external linkages, Bangladesh is prominent.

They are getting all supports and trainings from the country to keep alive their democratic struggle. Its cadres reportedly run camps and use Bangladeshi soil, particularly the jungles along the international border with India, to house hideouts. This was indicated by Church leaders, who mediated with top BNLF leaders at their hideouts in May 2000 for the release of two Mizoram government employees. The same was stated as early as in 1998 by the then Mizoram Chief Minister, Lalthanhawla. BNLF cadres who had survived the July 2000 internecine clashes with NLFT also confessed that they had hideouts in the Chittagong Hill Tracts (CHT).

BNLF established a strong linkages with other terrorist outfits operating in the northeast.It has very close links with the NLFT. It had even signed a 'Memorandum of Understanding' (MoU), which stipulated, *inter alia*, that the NLFT would provide arms, ammunition and all logistic support to the BNLF. Thus, the NLFT helped BNLF grow and gain in strength. This linkage was soured because of the BNLF's alleged pro-India tilt, its contacts with Indian security forces and for abducting and killing Christian employees and police personnel of Mizoram.

Eventually, it culminated in a bloody conflict in which approximately 75 BNLF cadres were killed by NLFT terrorists in a raid on a BNLF camp in Bangladesh. The then president and general secretary of BNLF were also taken hostage, but have now escaped from their captors and have since then surrendered to Indian security forces, as already mentioned.

Another bloody conflict occurred between the two outfits on September 3, 2000. 14 BNLF and 10 NLFT cadres were reportedly killed at a Bangladeshi hideout of the NLFT where it had invited BNLF to negotiate the release of their president and general secretary. Following these incidents, the BNLF-NLFT connection ended.

After its NLFT linkage turned sour, the BNLF came into contact with the National Socialist Council of Nagaland- Isak Muivah (NSCN-IM), which obliged the outfit by providing an unspecified number of AK 47 rifles and ammunition. The BNLF has also maintained contacts with the United Liberation Front of Asom (ULFA). This had also been revealed by then Chief Minister of Mizoram, Lalthanhawla, in 1998.

Current Situation

Currently, the BNLF is engaged in negotiations with the Mizoram government to settle the issues that it had raised. After few rounds of interactive talks, they have not been able to reach a solution yet. However, both sides have not given up hope and have agreed to continue with the talks.

The points of difference between the two sides relate to the determining the number of refugees who would be repatriated from Tripura, and the structure and nature of the political arrangement that should to be put on place after the returning refugees are rehabilitated. While the BNLF contends that the number of Reangs awaiting repatriation is more than 32,000, the Mizoram government holds that it is no more than a little over 10,000. On the kind of political arrangement that should follow, the BNLF has toned down its demand for an autonomous district council and is willing to negotiate for something less, a regional council.

The Mizoram government has refused to grant any separate autonomous governing body for the Reangs, so far. Moreover, the state government is also not ready to accept the BNLF's demand that the union government should be involved in the ongoing peace talks. The state government has also demanded that BNLF cadres should surrender if a lasting solution were to be found and peace restored in the region.[3]

BNLF is the major deterrent group to the peaceful return of Reangs. This was repeatedly raised by the Mizoram government at several platforms and meetings. In a meeting on 7 th August, 2000 held in Delhi attended by former Central Home Minister L.K. Advani, Tripura Chief Minister Manik Sarkar and Mizoram Home Minister Tawon Loiwa unanimously decided for the return of Reang refugees before October 16, 2000.But there was no sign of their return.

Mizoram government initially stepped the process because of BNLF's continuous terror activities. But later it disgreed to repatriate Reangs. This decision of the state government was criticised by political leaders, Bru committee and BNLF. In a joint statement it said that Zoramthanga was much more interested in resolving the terror problem in northeast than solving the problem of his own state.[4]

Since, he was meeting terrorist leaders of northeast and why he was unwilling to meet the leaders of BNLF, asked Reang leaders.

During first week of November, 2000 a team comprising of 15 – 20 militants entered the area of Khajura village near Baruncherra of Hailakandi district, a media report confirmed them as BNLF militants. They collected Rs. 300 from each family of around 700 families. They threatened to kill the villagers if deny to pay the funds demanded. These militants lifted many valuable items, cattles belonging to the villagers. However, the activity of the militants had created a greater panic among the villagers at the bordering areas of Assam and Tripura adjacent to Mizoram.

When their repatriation observed iffy, BNLF started approaching Mizoram government. It had further sent a memorandum to Chief Minister Zoramthanga, demanding of an autonomous council to implement developmental schemes for Reang dominated areas in Mizoram. MPs from Tripura also raised the Reang issue and criticized Mizoram government's reluctance to take back Reang refugees from Tripura refugee camps.

Bru and BNLF leaders repeatedly demanded for autonomy in Mizoram.But the authority in Aizawl made the situation more complex. There was a strict adherance that the proposal for repatriation of Reang refugees would not be completed until the Reang insurgents surrender their arms and create a conductive atmosphere in the state.[5]

When government was calm to its decision, BNLF had decided to surrender its arms and ammunitions. A group of terrorists surrendered to Assam Rifle under the leadership Suryamoni Reang on September 2001.[6]

Mizoram government further claimed that BNLF was alive and active. To prove it, it has engaged Mizoram Bru Welfare Association to establish the fact that– BNLF was operating. A donation of Rs. 25 lakhs was sourced from Mizo political leaders, which was utilised for training of Reang youths, taken them from Kanchanpur refugee camps and sent to Chittagong Hill Tracts (Bangladesh) for militant training, channeled through Mizoram Bru Welfare Association, a media report confirmed.

BNLF was further divided into two parts. The new organisation Bru Liberation Front of Mizoram (BLFM) floted, kept them away and created a new militancy base station at Bhuban Hills of Cachar district in Assam. It further started operating with 25 members, led by Lalmun Fela.

A meeting was held on 16 March, 2002 in between BNLF leaders and Chief Secretary of Mizoram. But that failed to bring any prosperous result on the return of Reang refugees. Mizoram government denied to establish a district council and neither they will provide any reservation in Assembly.

Bilateral discussions between government and BNLF leaders earlier took place in several occasions. BNLF strictly maintained that their demands to be fulfilled in the direction of self- governance and autonomy. The leaders of BNLF wanted central government to join the ongoing negotiation process, as there was no outcome of any demands being accepted by Mizo government.

Observing that there was no sign of progress of the negotiation,BNLF started asking a third party to intervene into the problem, particularly the Centre to held the dialogue and mitigate. Mizoram government refused any third party involvement in this negotiation. BNLF militants had surrendered with a pre-condition that Mizo government would resolve the Reang problem. But nothing has occurred in that direction.

There was an announcement of another meeting on 10 April, 2002 within surrendered BNLF leaders and Mizo government. But that too came with bearish results. All sections of the society wanted that Reang refugees should come back to their homeland. Christian missionaries in Mizoram also wanted its early solution. But Mizoram government always appeared with hard bargain, *"how many will return"*.

It had earlier decided that only 16 thousand Reang refugees of Tripura were the citizens of Mizoram. And, rest refugees in the refugee camps came from Tripura. The way the Mizoram goverment is dealing the problem that will raze the process of negotiation. The dealy in negotiating the Reang problem will creat more disturbance within the society. During my visit to the refugee camps they had discussed the weal and woe of Reang refugees, saying that, "we can't deny the possibility of further actions by BNLF against state government with arms and ammunitions. And this can pose a serious threat to the Mizo society.

NOTES

1. Reangs (Bru) demands separate identity. *The Sentinel*, Guwahati. March 28, 2000.
2. It is impossible to bring back Reangs, if BNLF continues arm terrorism: Zoramthanga, September, 2000.
3. www.satp.org [Internet].
4. Trouble in return to Mizoram, November, 4, 2000. Guwahati.
5. Reang autonomy heat on Mizoram government, *The Statesman*, June 10, 2001. Kolkata.
6. New plan of Mizo. Govt., not to return the Reangs, *Dainik Jugasankha*, January 20, 2002.

7 Role of NHRC, Central and State Governments in Reang Repartiation

The role of NHRC, central government and state governments, in the repartition of Reang refugees, in their immense stature, is very crucial. After receiving complaints, National Human Rights Commission (NHRC) sent an investigating team for overall assessment of the Reang trouble. On the basis of NHRC report, central government granted rations to the refugees. Before that, NHRC asked the central government to take adequate measures of the infiltrated Reangs of Mizoram. At times, it suggested both central and state governments to repatriate the Reang refugees.

The Mizoram government who once agreed to accept its disown people, when NHRC made a fervent approach. NHRC had been successful to apply the adequate pressures to both state governments, Mizoram and Tripura. It had asked both the governments to arrange their safe return. However, NHRC made the central government, state governments of Mizoram and Tripura bound to attend the problem. Many meetings were held to workout a solution for their repatriation. But the initiative seemed to have made rare progress. Yet—today the problem is not resolved. This chapter discussed the initiatives of NHRC, central and state governments.

The NHRC made its best efforts to minimise the painstaking Reang trouble within its limited function. NHRC can only enquire the violations of human rights; it can study the living conditions of the inmates and make necessary recommendations under the constitution or any law for the time being in force for the protection of human rights. It can step up for quick measures for their effective implementation. When the enquiry of commission comes to a conclusion that reflects the severe violation of human rights occurred, it can't by itself take any step to get the wrong undone, but it can recommend to the concerned government or central authority to initiate proceedings for prosecution or such other action or approach the supreme court or the high court concerned for such directions, orders or writs as the court may deem to the victims.

Monitoring the Situation by NHRC

The National Human Rights Commission (NHRC) has directed the Mizoram government to take back an estimated 40,000 Reang refugees living in Tripura, and asked the Centre to play an active role in arranging their repatriation on priority basis. The Commission held the view that "The Reangs living in refugee camps in Kanchanpur sub-division of Tripura are lawful inhabitants of Mizoram and the state government is obliged to take them back in accordance with the agreement made with the Union Home Minister in November 1997".

In a meeting in 1999 held by NHRC member Sudarshan Agarwal with chief secretaries of Mizoram, Tripura and Assam in Agartala, the commission said that the Mizoram government should take all necessary steps to impart a sense of confidence and security to the refugees who fled the state in the wake of ethnic tension in 1997. Regarding the number of refugees could be resolved by joint verification at the camps by a committee comprising representatives of Tripura and Mizoram governments and Union Home Ministry.

NHRC asked the Centre to play an active role in arranging repatriation of the Reangs to Mizoram in accordance with the decision taken in the meeting of Union Home Minister in November, 1997 and impart urgent attention to the safety and security of Reangs returning to their villages.[1]

Though in late remedial measures were taken by central government. Centre had supported all the Reangs through providing basic amenities such as regular supply of rice, dal, salt, cash dole, edible oil, dry fish, clothes, soap and others. Central government provided all these essential goods and materials only when NHRC had recommended central government for supplying rations and cash dole.

The delegates of NHRC visited twice at Reang refugee camps for assessment of Reang trouble. The major step of NHRC was to recognise them as refugees and in its second phase visit, it has criticized the government for their inadequate care, poor supply of drinking water and asked the government for sufficient and adequate measures.

Steps of the Central and State Governments

The Indian government insists that the Mizoram state government should provide the necessary conditions for the return of all Reangs displaced into Tripura state (2000). Mizos believe that the Reangs are outsiders and hence have no right to claim that they are permanent settlers. The Chief Minister of Mizoram argues that "Reangs were not original residents of Mizoram and that only 16,000 of the refugees have a valid claim to reside in the state.

Meanwhile, the Reangs are believed to be increasingly joining the insurgent groups, waging a holly war against the Mizos. The Indian government and the National Human Rights Commission has called on the Mizoram and Tripura state governments to assure the immediate and safe return of the Reangs.

On August 2000, decisions were taken that Reang refugees would be resettled in Tripura and the repatriation of the entire group would be completed by year's end, but nothing had been done to repatriate them by year's end.

The Mizoram government had sent a delegation led by the state Home Minister, in October, 1997 to persuade the Reangs living in camps in Tripura to return. A programme of repatriation was also chalked out with Tripura government. However, barring 3000 Reangs, most of them refused to return Mizoram even after the government promised to provide adequate security by deploying Central Paramilitary Forces in the area.

Citing the facts of the failure of Reang represation, the state Home Minister blamed the Bru Union saying that president of the Bru

Students Union, on March 9,1998 warned all the Reangs who had not left the state to leave the state by March 22,1998 or face excommunication by the community or even death.

The then Union Home Minister L.K. Advani during his visit to northeast on September, 1998 stated that " the Mizoram government must take back every Reang tribal now housed in relief camps in Tripura for whom the Centre is bearing the expenses and there was no question of taking back selectively". He rejected the former Chief Minister Lal Thanhawla's assertion that he would take back only those Reang tribals whose names were in Mizoram electoral rolls.

The Reangs living in camps have demanded guaranteed protection from the Mizoram government as a precondition for their return to their homeland.

The Mizos believe that the Reangs are rank outsiders and hence have no right to claim that they are permanent settlers. The former Chief Minister of Mizoram, Lal Thanhawla in a statement had said that "Reangs were not original residents of Mizoram and they had crossed over to Mizoram areas from Tripura and the Chittagong Hill Tracts of Bangladesh in search of land for jhum cultivation and that his government had no obligation to take back the Reangs." The Reangs are believed to be increasingly joining the insurgent groups to wage war against the Mizos.

NHRC Delegation Visit in Reang Camps

A high level delegation of the National Human Rights Commission (NHRC) visited the Reang camps in Tripura. The delegation members talked to the Reang leaders and also with the state officials in Tripura regarding problems of the Reangs.

Later, on the basis of delegation's report the NHRC wrote to the Mizoram Chief Secretary "to make necessary arrangements without any further delay so that they could go back to their villages in Mizoram. Reangs living in camps were residents of Mizoram and that it was the responsibility of the state government to arrange their immediate repatriation." The Union Government has also requested the Mizoram authorities for taking necessary steps for early return of the Reangs. [2]

A report said that the Reang tribal group from Mizoram has been displaced due to a sectarian conflict presently is being sheltered in 6 refugee camps in north Tripura; conditions in such camps are poor and the Tripura government has asked the central government to allot funds for their care.

Reang leaders in the camps said to this author that their community would return to Mizoram if they were granted an autonomous district council, allotted a set number of seats in the Mizoram Assembly, and granted financial assistance for resettlement. The Mizoram government, however, rejected these demands and maintained that only 16,000 of the refugees had a valid claim to reside in the state.

Several discussions held between the central government and state governments of Tripura and Mizoram on repatriation of displaced Reangs. On 7 August 2000, former Union Home Minister of L.K. Advani held a meeting with Chief Minister, Tripura, Manik Sarkar and former Mizoram Home Minister, Tawnluia to discuss the problem of repatriation of displaced Reangs from Mizoram who were settled in camps inside Tripura. Union Home Secretary, Additional Secretary (Home), Chief Secretary, Tripura and Joint Secretary (north east) in the Union Home Ministry were also present. It was noted that the National Human Right Commission in October 1999 after discussions with the state governments of Mizoram and Tripura and the representatives of Ministry of Home Affairs and after the visits to the camps, had made the following observations.

1. The Reangs living in refugee camps in Kanchanpur sub-division of Tripura are lawful inhabitants of Mizoram and the government of Mizoram is obliged to take them back in accordance with the agreement made with the Union Home Minister in November, 1997. The government of Mizoram should take all necessary steps in impart a sense of confidence and security to the refugees who fled from Mizoram in the wake of some ethnic tension in September-October, 1997. Dispute, if any, regarding the number of refugees, can be resolved by joint verification at the camps by a committee comprising the representatives of government of Tripura and

Mizoram and the Ministry of Home Affairs who would consult fully with a representative of the Reang refugees.

2. The government of India is requested to play active role on priority basis to arrange repatriation of the Reangs to Mizoram in accordance with the decision taken in the meeting of Union Home Minister in November, 1997. The ministry of Home Affairs is further requested to impart urgent and special attention to the safety and security of the Reangs returning to their villages in Mizoram.
3. The Ministry of Home Affairs, government of India, state government of Mizoram and Tripura shall keep the Commission informed of the progress made in the matter at regular intervals of atleast once in two months.
4. It was noted that there were 31151 displaced Reangs (6956 families) in these Camps in Tripura. Government of Tripura informed that they had sent the full details of the displaced persons to district authorities in Mizoram for verification.
5. Representatives of the government of Mizoram agreed that they had received the list on 7 July, 2000 and the process of verification is on.
6. It was urged by the Union Home Minister that the verification should be expedited and the process of repatriation commenced at the earliest.

After discussions, the following decisions were taken: -

1. The first phase of repatriation of 16000 displaced persons verified by the government of Mizoram who have been displaced from Mizoram would be completed by 30 October, 2000.
2. In the second phase, there would be further verification of balance person left in the camps and thereafter, such of those who were found to have been displaced from Mizoram would be repatriated back by 31 December, 2000.
3. Simultaneously tripartite talks would be held between government of India, government of Mizoram and Reang representatives to bring about a settlement of outstanding issues and an end to violence[3].

On August 7, 2000 following his meeting with Tripura Chief Minister Manik Sarkar, former Union Home Minister L.K. Advani announced that an initial group of Reang refugees would be resettled in Tripura by October 31, 2000 and that repatriation of the entire group would be completed by year's end. However, while an NHRC staff member also visited Tripura to inquire into the situation of the Reangs, by year's end nothing had been done to repatriate them.

Some recommendations for the successful return of the Reangs to Mizoram state (2000):

"The government of Mizoram had shown reluctance in accepting all the Reangs living in camps in the past. Both the central government and the NHRC have given categorical directions to the state government of Mizoram to accept all the Reangs but the directions have not yet been complied. The fact that the state government has also ignored the directions of NHRC is quite serious. Concerted efforts of the state and the central government can only bring about their return. Most of the Reangs would return to their villages if proper security arrangements are made. In order to assure them that no harm would come to them, such security arrangements should continue for sufficiently long period of time. It would be necessary to take strong action against the insurgent outfit "the Bru National Army" who would try by all means to prevent their return.

It would be necessary to provide adequate assistance to the Reangs on their return. They have demanded that adequate compensation should be paid for the houses which have been destroyed during the generalized violence. As the Reangs are basically dependent on subsistence agriculture in the hilly terrain and their economic conditions being very poor, it would be necessary to continue the assistance now being given in relief camps for few months after their return." [4]

Discussions Between Governments

When pressures exerted on Mizoram government by central government, the officials of Mizoram government made their formal visit to the camps in Tripura. The delegation team accompanied by Mizoram Home Minister and some other government officials visited the refugee camps on 1st November 1997. The then Tripura Home Minister also visited with the Mizo delegates. Both governments had discussed about their save return in Mizoram. But the discussions in between two governments even were more or less fruitful. In the second week of November 1997 three thousand Reangs returned to Mizorm. But they further came back to refugee camps in absence of their proper security arrangement.

A discussion on November 11, 1997 was held in New Delhi by the invitation of Central Home Minister L.K. Advani attended by the high level official home ministry of Tripura and Mizoram government. In Delhi the discussion was emphasized on the safe return of Reang refugees and the whole thrust of the discussion was that Mizoram government immediately start the process of their safety returns in Mizoram with adequate security.

The Mizoram Deputy Commissioner comprising a Mizo delegation had further visited the Tripura refugee camps on November 30; 1997.They discussed with the Reang leaders for their return. In that point of time Reang leaders even agreed returning to Mizorm. But finally Reang leaders refused to return in the fear that their life will be in danger and violence may further perpetuate in Reang villages. A team of Mizo police and AIG visited the camps and asked them to return but the Reangs denied returning in that unsure situation.

Dispute on Legal Reang Residents

Disagreement over the definition of legal residents of Mizoram is a major impediment in returning of the Reang displaced population, presently living in relief camps in Tripura (2001). The government of Mizoram claimed to have completed the process of identifying the "legal" Reang residents of Mizoram and have placed the figure at a little over 10,000.The government of Tripura maintains that the actual number is over 31,000. Both the state government of Tripura and the union government urged the state government of Mizoram to expedite the return of the displaced persons. Repatriation of Bru / Reangs from Tripura camps should not be implemented until the Bru National Liberation Front (BNLF) laid down arms, this is what the Mizoram Home Minister used to say later.

"The state government claims to have completed the process of identifying the "legal" Reang residents of Mizoram and have placed the figure at a little over 10,000, according to a report of UNI. With this, the Mizoram administration has literally rubbished the claims made by Tripura that over 31,000 Reangs living in the northern refugee camps belonging to the state. The announcement could have far reaching effect on the demographic profile of the region, as Mizoram can now refuse entry to over 20,000 Reangs / Brus who were claiming to be residents of the state. Placing the Reangs under two categories, the state administration claimed that while 10,142 refugees now languishing in Tripura refugee camps were the original residents of Mizoram, the rest had come from Assam, and parts of Tripura itself.

According to the Mizoram government, while 8,396 Reangs were the residents of the Aizawl district, 1,746 belonging to the southern district of Lunglei. Aizawl Deputy Commissioner claimed that the list prepared by the administration was based on records and not interviews. "Therefore, any Reang who could produce sufficient, documentary evidence on his citizenship would be added to the list," he said, adding that the administration had exhausted all means of identifying more people.

On August 1999, Agartala had sent a list of 31,600 Reang residents of Mizoram living in refugee camps in Tripura. But, according to the state government, since the list did not mention the details of their villages, subdivisions, Assembly segments and polling station, the administration failed to trace their antecedents. The state Home department of Mizoram then referred the matter to Tripura government asking for complete details of their claims.

During 1997-98, thousands Reang refugees had fled to Tripura fearing repression from Mizos after a forest game watcher was killed by suspected Reang rebels in October 1997. The Mizoram government has so far maintained that the Reangs were forced to leave Mizoram by the Bru National Liberation Front (BNLF), a Reang militant outfit, demanding an autonomous district council for Reangs."[5]

"The Chief Minister of Tripura Manik Sarkar maintained that he had discussed with Union Home Minister L K Advani about the 30,000 Bru / Reangs, temporarily sheltered in north Tripura district, during his early visit to New Delhi. According to Sarkar, Advani expressed dissatisfaction over the Mizoram government not taking any steps to solve the longstanding problem. "We have given shelter to Bru/Reangs on a humanitarian ground and how long one can provide help to them", the Chief Minister asked. While Tripura government claimed that 31,919 Reangs belonging to 6,114 families fled Mizoram and were in six camps, Mizoram government further contended that it could identify only 11,015 belonging to 1,627 families as bonafide residents of Mizoram.

Mizoram Home Minister previously expressed his concern that repatriation of Brus/Reangs from Tripura camps should not be implemented until the Bru National Liberation Front (BNLF) laid down arms. He said, the government turned down the BNLF proposal to hold tripartite talks involving the union home ministry as the issues were under the purview of the state."[6] The central government questions the position of the Mizoram authorities: "The Reang problem persists without any solution and the government of Mizoram has, however, not shown the desired urgency to implement the decisions. The continued presence of a large number of displaced Reangs from Mizoram in camps in Tripura is a security threat to both Tripura and Mizoram."

There are reports of recruitment of idle youth who are getting increasingly frustrated from the camps to the ranks of the Bru National Liberation Force (BNLF), a BRU militant group. The state government of Mizoram would need to expedite the return of the displaced persons to bring normalcy to the state."[7]

Since June 11, 1998 Bru National Union (BNU) leaders had in several occassions met the Mizoram Chief Minister and discussed its early solution, and the discussions has no final outcome.

During October 1999, NHRC delegates visited Tripura and on October, 11 of the year the Additional Secretary of central government, Chief Secretary of Assam and Tripura attended a meeting at Tripura on the problem of Reangs' repatriation but left with many holes. Further on 5 & 6 June, 2000 in another meeting attended by central home ministry Secretary Ajay Srivastava and delegates of Mizoram and Tripura governments.[8] All of them failed to concede a final decision of Reang's problem to a agreeable point, ended with further uncertainty of Reang repatriation issue.

Process of Repatriation

It has become the greatest impediment of Reangs' return to their home when Mizoram government enunciated their unclear decision on Reang repatriation. The decision of the government was very ambiguous in character,there was no sterm steps exactly when they will be repatriated. Mizoram Home Secretary had earlier assured in a high level meeting in New Delhi in the year 1898 that Mizoram government would take all necessary steps for the safe return of nearly 18,000 Reang refugees at first phase (32,000 or 40,000 it was a point of contradiction) who fled to either Tripura or south Assam's Hailakandi district.

The Mizoram government has ignored the decision arrived in a meeting in-between the Union Home Minister L.K. Advani, Tripura Chief Minister Manik Sarkar and Mizoram Chief Minister Zoramthanga for completing the process of their first phase repatriation of Reang evacuees. In a meeting in New Delhi on August 7,2000, the Mizoram government was told by the centre to complete Reang repatriation in the first phase on or before October 30,2000. [9]

The Tripura government send a list of 16,000 names of the evacuees along with necessary particulars to the Mizoram's district administration at Mammith to hasten repatriation process, but Mizoram government returned the list to Tripura government with a request to mention specific details about each of the evacuees and the polling stations in Mizoram where they had earlier exercised their franchisee during elections.

The Tripura government had revised list the according to the demand of the Mizoram government on October,21 2000, so that the process of sending back Reang evacuees could begin immediately. The authority in Mizoram was conspicuous by their silence over the next course of action to be taken up. Mizoram government spurned the plea of Tripura government's decision of early return and preferred not to communicate to Tripura government on the decision of first phase repatriation by October 30,2000.

During the time there were around 35,000 Reang evacuees huddled in six different camps in Kanchanpur and Dasda region of north Tripura. Central government had to made huge investment for their shelter and feeding the refugees, just in providing the food and relief, the government expenditure went upto 22 crores on October, 2000.

After a long silence Mizoram Chief Minister Zoramthanga once announced that Reang refugees were not the citizens of his state. He further added that it was not an obligation for his government to take back the Reang evacuees. Reacting to his statement the Tripura's Chief Minister Manik Sarkar strongly refuted and further asked him to repatriate the Reang refugees.

Later on NHRC also wrote a letter to the Mizoram Chief Secretary urging his government to arrange for taking back the Reang refugees on the earliest. The union home ministry persuaded the Mizoram government in a couple of occasions to initiate the process of repatriation. Mizoram government later diverted their attention to a separate issue, saying that government will not repatriate the Reangs unless they abdicate insurgency and if Reang insurgent group continue to shun violence in north-east.

The decision of the government severally criticised in various platforms, when government tickled down the Reang repatriation. Bru National Union and Bru Refugee Committee had said that the Mizoram government and Chief Minister were wholly responsible in the process of repatriation. The political wings in Tripura and NGOs also criticized the government comdemning it a "baseless and senseless". The BNU and BRC were sought for centre and NHRC help in their repatriation.

Failure of Repatriation Process

The reluctance of Mizoram government in Reang repatriation when seen in great appearance, few Reangs swelled the ranks of rioters and the Reang terrorists became active in the Tripura-Mizoram border. The known militant outfit of Reangs, BNLF had started pressuring on Mizoram government for granting autonomy to the minority Reang tribesmen in the state. The BNLF leaders have sent a memorandum to the Mizoram Chief Minister Zoramthanga, demanding demarcation of an autonomous region for the minority Reangs in the state and setting up an autonomous council to implement developmental schemes for Mizoram's Reang dominated areas. At the same time the Reang politicians and organisations were exerting pressures on centre in the line to protect the rights of Reang tribesmen in the state.

A home ministry report said that the government of Tripura and Mizoram had reasons to worry if the authority in Aizawl did not solve the Reang problem. Members of Parliament from Tripura have also expressed their concern in Parliament in Delhi over Mizoram government's apathy to return Reang refugees.

But at last, Mizoram government made it clear that the repatriation of Reang evacuees will not start until Reang insurgents surrender their arms and create a congenial atmosphere for peace in the state. The authorities in Aizawl later informed the Tripura government that only 10,000 camp inmates were the genuine citizens of Mizoram and the rest were infiltrated from Tripura and Bangladesh. Tripura government expressed strong resentments against the Mizoram government's stance and asked the centre for applying adequate pressure on the Mizoram government for early repatriation of the refugees.

What Tripura government earlier had sent a list of Reang residents of Mizoram living in refugee camps in Tripura that was strictly refused on the basis of following claims: since the list did not mention the details of their villages, subdivisions, Assembly segments and polling station, the administration failed to trace their antecedents.

The State Home department then referred the matter to Tripura asking for complete details of the claimants. During 1997-98, several thousand Reangs had fled to Tripura fearing repression from Mizos after a forest game watcher was killed by suspected Reang rebels in October 1997. The Mizoram government has so far maintained that the Reangs were forced to leave Mizoram because of the Bru National Liberation Front (BNLF), a Reang militant outfit, demanding an autonomous district council for Reangs.[10]

Earlier in a meeting in New Delhi called by Prime Minister attended by Chief Ministers of northeast in which Mizoram Chief Minister Zoramthanga brought a strong allegation before Prime Minister saying that Reangs were active in breaking the peace process in the state. A home ministry source in Mizoram said that Reangs were involved in killing of four Christian missionaries on April 25, 2000.This allegation even been notified to central home ministry. Mizoram Home Minister Tawanluia even requested to central ministry to ban Bru organisation under the 1969 security Act.[11]

When Mizoram government refuted the Reang repatriation and maintained its early stance – "surrender the Reang militants first and then repatriation". On September 2001, the BNLF troop led by Surya

Mani Reang surrendered to Assam Rifles. The government excuse didn't end there; Mizo government denied the surrender in full and said that the BNLF exists. To stop the repatriation of Reangs, Mizoram government insisted a group of Reangs in Mizoram namely Mizo Bru welfare Association to re-forge the Reang militant outfits, this time which was allegedly said to have the total support of Mizoram government in the line of paying Rs.25 lakhs to that welfare organisation and through them to prove the fact that Reang insurgency is alive and active.[12] After a prolong negotiations and discussions the situation is quite clear that Mizoram government is not willing to repatriate the Reang refugees anymore, and it has been changing its stance from one issue to another, time and again. Earlier government was telling that refugees were not the citizens of Mizoram except 10,000 among them .It had further claimed that government will not repatriate unless Reang militants surrender and when Reang militants surrendered it has changed its decision and kept on proving that Reang militants are active, a new militant organisation, on behalf of Reangs, was created, non-officially grants came to Reang leaders from the state itself to continue terrorism.

Fresh Initiatives and Discussions

In a fresh delegates meeting at Delhi on March 15, 2001 headed by Additional Home Secretary at the centre had fixed a date May 31, 2001, within which refugees will be taken back to Mizoram, as signed by the Mizoram and Tripura Chief Secretaries.[13] At there, Mizoram government raised the similar excuse that all the sheltered Reangs in Refugee camps were not the Reangs originated from Mizoram. It has, however, further perplexed the Reang trouble.

In a meeting on March 16, 2002 held in between Mizoram government and surrendered BNLF and Reang leaders, government had further re-cleared its stance that government will not support on the issue of creation of an autonomous council and reservation of Reang representation in state assembly. Reang leaders were thinking on the direction that after surrendering of BNLF militants, government will cooperate and will agree on their demands. But their idea didn't work. Not only they refuged its latest decision, Mizoram government informed to the Reang leaders that apart from the demand of Autonomous Council and without any reservation in Assembly if they agree to come back in the state then Mizoram government will have no objection in their repatriation. Reang leaders refused the government's restand and they emphasised their demands.

In its second phase of discussion with Reang leaders, a meeting was held in Aizwal on March 16, 2002 attended by Mizoram Chief Secretary and surrendered BNLF Home Secretary (self made) Zaithanga Apeto and his other delegates. On behalf of the government it had set the pre-condition for the return of refugees. The first and foremost one was that all BNLF militants have to surrender. On the other hand surrendered BNLF had made 10 point conditions before the government for their repatriation. It said that the Reang dominated west-Aizwal should be declared as Reang autonomous council. Five assembly seats should have to be reserved for Reang population, re-include the name of Reang voters in the election list, Reangs have to be repatriated in Mizoram, the surrendered BNLF outfits have to be resettled. In all, the government disagreed with the demands placed by Reangs. There were many such meetings and talks held in-between government of Mizoram and Reang leaders.

The relentless incidents of violence, gang rape and torture on Reang villagers in Mizoram with arms and ammunitions by Mizo youths is a glaring example: how the rights of Reangs have been sullied. "We can't blame any particular individual or organisation. But the Mizoram government is wholly responsible in those attacks. Majority Mizos came with heavy arms and ammunitions in Reang villages and killed many innocent Reang villagers. Organizations like MSA, MZP, MAP held attacks on us. We had the population of 85 thousand in Mizoram and around 52 thousand left the state in Mizo attacks. The helpless Reangs came down to Tripura and Assam, maintained their livelihood without government help. And some of them mingled with local Reangs in Tripura and few fled away to Bangladesh. The series of house burning incidents and killing the Reangs were stopped when NHRC and central government have taken up the matter seriously. The harassments are still continued in Mizoram", informed Bruno Msha, President of MBRC. The saddest part of our life is that – being the citizens of this country we, the Reangs, have been stripped from our fundamental rights. We are supposed to get all facilities as like other citizens of this country. But Reangs were treated as rubble people in the state. "We still hope to lead a normal life if government supports. We would like to return to our homeland as early as possible. The situation has taken a complex turn and ours is not a peripheral concern. This time we can only return if Mizoram government takes the initiative," averred Lalduhawma Chorkhy, Joint Secretary and In-charge information and publicity, MBRC.

Unchange Ground Situation

Despite of several attempts of NHRC, central government and Tripura government it failed to convince the Mizoram government for the repatriation Reang refugees. That has not changed the ground situation. It was seen as the less political initiative in Mizoram. State government, however, realised that if they start accepting Reangs, and allows them to repatriate – this will definitely hurt the sentiment of majority Mizos—which was an unwelcome decision of Mizo government. There was a fear that, this little issue could pull back the government from power. So, the best way was to deviate the issue what a policy Mizoram government adopted later, and Reang issue couldn't perpetuate into any big controversy in the state. Analysts say that government will never take such a drastic step at least for their greater interest to remain in power.

"The demand of autonomous council and reservation of seats in assembly, if maintained, Mizoram government will not be in a position to accept these. The Reangs, if, don't step down from their early decision, repatriation is not possible", believes Uttam Chakma, former SDO, Kanchanpur sub-division in Tripura.

Tripura government is not willing to bear the burden of Reang refugees anymore. Government intention is to send back the Reangs as early as possible. Some of the Reang evacuees in the camps have decided to settle down in Tripura. Because, they are getting government relief and all basic amenities. The Tripura government's intention is to reduce the services further and in trouble they will decide to move to other places. Otherwise, Reangs could settle down in Tripura." observed Harihar Prasad, Assistant Organization Secretary,Kalyan Ashram ,Tripura.

The parameter of the problem is very distinct— if they are identified as the people of Mizoram, they will have the full right to exercise their fundamental rights and they can go back to their own state. The question is—under what condition they can go back to Mizoram. The unwilling grueling attitude of the Mizoram government to accept them has to be changed first. The central government supports all their accommodation and fooding in Tripura. The major question is their social acceptability and the changing attitude of the Mizo people. Can it be changed or not? This is the more serious issue of present days.

At this point of time, it is more important to understand whether they will be accepted in Mizoram. The statistics, of how many people are willing to go and how many people of migrated Reangs will be taken back, does not bear any importantance. It is simply the statistics of politics is going on in-between Mizoram and Tripura government. Who is held responsible that can't be shrugged. The number can be systematized more accurately, and can be corrected during the physical repatriation process; who is eligible to go back or who is not eligible. The process of repatriation should begin as early as possible.

It is, of course, the majority people in Mizoram have to show the bengaminity, and at the same time Reangs have the political aspirations must be accommodated to the extent to consider it legitimate and considering the possible areas. It is not going to solve the Reang problem, if it is argued just to say that Chakmas have the autonomy, Maras and Lais have the autonomous district councils and Reangs should have the similar pattern of autonomy.

The best possible way to solve this problem is that when central government will chalk out a solution, in a very effective manner. Or some political arrangements may be made between Mizoram and Tripura government. It is also possible that Reang might be integrated in Tripura state.

There are more dangerous aspects may rattle if repatriation is done by force or by putting pressure on the Mizoram government. It is the question of the security of Reang tribes. Some sort of public opinion may be build in the state, in favour of Reang repatriation process,then the chances of their accommodation are much brighter in Mizoram. In question to their security and safety, it is not only the responsibility of the central government but also the Mizoram government and local community have to ponder over. An inter -

community relationship should have to be built within diversified tribal groups.

Enforcing laws or imposing pressure on Mizoram government will not solve the entire problem either. It may create adverse situation and entire community may clash each other. It can only be solved with proper negotiations and holding dialogues. But unfortunately, it is taking much time ahead on this issue. This is in general a human problem. We have no immediate solution to address the problem. The negotiations are going on and they are only failing.

It is the failure of inter community relationship and it cannot be addressed by legal measures. It is the question of social acceptability in Mizoram. Although, a part of Reang people have been invited in Mizoram.If they don't find any security in Mizoram they maybe settled in Tripura. Tripura government is also going to be more insensitive in their long-term pressure, and realising it overburden to its economy. Now the two options are open with the government – either a sort of community relationship should be built up or refugees should be settled in Tripura.

The major reasons for which Reang refugees are unable to stay in Mizoram are:

(a) General awareness about basic rights among Reang society.
(b) Discrimination on the basis of religion.
(c) Sporadic treatment in implementation of government programs in Reang dominated areas in Mizoram.
(d) Demand of autonomous district as remedy upon these problems.

"The situation of the Reang refugees has become very tardy and serious from every point of view. The refugees are becoming very lazy in comfort living and adopted a selfish lifestyle. The fear of asphyxiation still exists in their minds and their attitude has become very acrid. They were taken in isolated refugee camps at where they have no work, no education and no such thinking to lead a prosperous life. Neither they are thinking for any development. In absence of proper medical facility their health condition is also derogating", said S.R. Vhide, Kalyan Ashram,Tripura.

Reangs are not encouranged to participate in the government

discussions and to hold their views. Vhide believes, "providing aids and other facilities are not the solution to this problem. They were much happy when central government supported them, but now their mental conditions started ruining and becoming more serious when they saw that central government and NHRC orders were not adhered by Mizoram government. Government is incapable to take back Reang refugees as because of the religious bigotry, political gains and the fear to fight against the vast religious group– Mizo-Christians–the majority of the population in Mizoram."

Reangs have very marginal voice in northeast and in absence of any political representation in northeast their voice never reaches to centre and other human rights organisations. All that compounded a great problem in their repatriation process. Presently there is no conflict except the controversy over the number of refugees sheltered in the camps. Tripura government believes that the population of Reang refugees will be around 32,000, and as per the Mizoram government it will be in between 10,000—20,000.If the repatriation of the Reang refugees is not possible in Mizoram, central government can divert some financial grants from Mizoram government to Trupura government, in proportionate to the population of the Reang refugees. The refugees can be settled in smaller groups in different villages all over Tripura. They should get citizenship, ration card and some helps so that Reangs could start their normal life and enjoy their fundamental rights provided by the constitution.

NOTES

1. Mizoram asked to take back Reang refugees, *Vol. 2 Issue 29-30,* Dec.7-Dec.21, 1999, www.nenanews.com
2. K.C. Saha, 2000, p.7-8, UN Guiding Principles on Internal Displacements: A Case Study of Internally Displaced Reangs of Mizoram in North-Estern India, [Views expressed in this paper are the author's personal] [Internet].
3. Ministry of Home Affairs, Government of India, (MHA-GoI), 7 August 2000, "Union Home Minister holds talks on the Reang issue" [Internet]
4. Mizoram ignores Reang return deadlines, October, 30,2000. *The Statesmen.*
5. *The Assam Tribune*, 21 March 2001, "Only 10,000 Reangs bonafide resident".

6. "Centre's assurance on Bru/Reangs problem" Times of India, 4 August 2001.
7. GOI, *Annual Report, 2000*.
8. Rs. 22 Crore granted for Reang refugee camps, *Dainik Jugasankha,* 16 July, 2000.
9. Mizoram ignores Reang return deadlines, October, 30,2000. *The Statesmen*. Home Ministry press release, *04.08.2000*.
10. The Assam Tribune, Guwahati, Wednesday, March 21, 2001
11. It is impossible to bring back Reangs, if BNLF continues arm terrorism,: Zoramthanga, *Jainik Jugasankha*, 8 Sept. 2000.
12. New plan of Mizo. Govt. not to return the Reangs, *Dainik Jugasankha*, 20 January 2002.
13. In the rollback of Government policy, Reangs are dilly- dallying, *Dainik Jugasankaha*, June 14, 2001. Guwahati.

8 Tribal Rights and Human Rights

Human rights – is an ancient concept in our country. It is a universal phenomenon, as old as humanity. The rights are fundamental to human existence. Human rights are those rights without which none can live with dignity. These rights are not privileges, nor gifts given at the whim of a ruler or a government. These cannot be taken away by any arbitrary power.

India signed the UN Declaration of Human Rights in 1948. In 1950, we adopted the constitution of India incorporating part-III on fundamental rights of citizens. The preamble, fundamental rights and the directive principles of state policy provide the provisions for basic human rights for our people (e.g. article 14, 15, 20, 21, 22, 32 etc.) We have many Indian acts in addition to Supreme Court judgements directing implementations of human rights provisions. We also have article 51(A) – fundamental duties – telling us that rights and duties have a very deep and direct connection. Many laws like Protection of Human Rights Act 1993; National Commission for Minorities Act, 1992; National Commission Women Act, 1990; Protection of Civil Rights Act, 1955; Scheduled and Scheduled Tribes (Prevention of Atrocities) Act, 1989; exist in India.

Good Governance in Democracy

The promotion and protection of human rights is possible only with good governance – reflected by a firm commitment to policies of equity and justice. With good governance rights of each citizen are respected everywhere and there is no place for organized cruelty, 'Pogroms' and 'ethnic cleansing'. In any democracy, good governance can occur only when each of its three pillars – the legislative, the executive and judiciary function with international standards and integrity. The element of good governance can be measured by quality and level of concern of governments for public good, respect for human rights of its citizens and the degree of political freedom and people's participation in the affairs of the state. And the key pillar-the parliament, can contribute a lot for a state-society relationship based on reciprocity and accountability.

The insurgency in northeast of India is the result of persistent injustice and unfair practices by the people in power, while dealing with public services. Restoration of peace is essential but this can only be achieved only with full respect of human rights coupled with proper political measures, which are truly democratic in character. Insurgency and terrorism can be wiped out only when we ensure that the rule of law prevails. This is possible if there is clear dialogue between policy makers, parliamentarians and legislators and the human rights proponents of our area.

Relative party strength is important but attitude and behaviour of political parties having concern for creative culture of human rights – already propagated by thinkers like Sankardev and Guru Nanak about 500 years ago in this country. Sankardev rightly taught us that injustice anywhere is a threat to justice everywhere as he found that his human rights movement faces challenges from the vested interests and the existing oppressive system.

In the words of Mahatma Gandhi, 'All humanity is one undivided and indivisible family and each one of us is responsible family and each one of us is responsible for the misdeeds of all the other. I can not detach myself from the wickedest soul.'

In Gandhian terms, taking care of healthy village self-government and the country's patriotic progress will take care of itself. To sum up, history, geography and cultural anthropology demand decentralized and democratic organs of justice, not haphazardly but on a planned basis, not condescendingly but ideologically.

Dealing with justice, the national leadership, the planning commission and the constitution Article 40 must pay homage to the nation by panchyat participation in social justice. The goal of development is not merely measuring the GNP but improving the dignity, status and opportunity of the individual. The central concern of our socialist republic is man; his responsibility and opportunity to manifest his divinity. Thus the quest for social justice coincides with rising the quality of human life and if our human members are huddled in hubble habitats in tribal rural India, development in its distributive strategy, must reach out to our villages. Justice to the villager is pivotal to distribute justice. And the problems of access and involvement are crucial to success. [1]

Former President of India K.R. Narayanan once mentioned, "fifty years into our life in the republic we find that justice – social, economic and political – remains an unrealised dream for millions of our fellow citizens. . . . Not surprisingly there is sullen resentment among the masses against their condition erupting often in violent forms in several parts of the country . . . many a social upheaval can be traced to the neglect of the lowest tier of society whose discontent moves towards the path of violence". [2]

Good government requires good policies – and government depends not only on state structures but also on political parties, as they have key functions in democracy. There is urgent need to improve the way political parties work – as they are a crucial part of the national civil society – as they transfer values into actions. Today we need good governance that is pro-active, not simply reactive- and we need leader made strong by vision, sustained by ethics and revealed by political courage that looks beyond the next election. [3]

India being the democratic country and its government must protect the rights of its citizens – the right to security of life, justice, equally before law, right to live, freedom of speech, freedom of religion, and getting relief from poverty etc. which are also fundamental rights. But over a majority of tribal people in northeast live in poverty. They are facing unending sufferings like illiteracy, economic instability, gender inequality, social discrimination, criminalisation of politics etc rendering the mass people helpless spectators over the selfishness of a politically corrupt leadership and the government as a whole.

India is welfare state and its government is a welfare government. So its people have every right to expect from it effective and healthy welfare programmes for all round development, at all levels. As such our fundamental rights need strong protection by the government. [4]

According to the assessment of fifty years' performance of the governments in northeast, politicians and opportunists having their vested interests in and outside of government's function have totally massacred the rights of tribal people. Most of the political leaders who have got the opportunity to run the government have involved in corruption and siphoned out public funds for their personal welfare.

Human rights do not discriminate the people on ground of religion, caste, creed, sex, and nationality rather they promote the equality of living of everyone.

Fundamental Rights

In such critical crisis of protection of human rights and civil liberty, we can claim our judiciary to be the only alternative which is the most powerful wing of the constitution and which can have a proper check on the ongoing criminal and antisocial activities perpetuated by the bad elements of the society. If certain aspects of the judiciary like speedy disposal of cases, appointment of strong judicial minded judges, abrogation of age-old long procedural laws, facilitating law commission to bring about healthy legal reforms in Indian laws, judicious expertise of the discriminatory provision of bail if are taken care of, then the human rights can be rightly protected for the larger interest of our society.

The fundamental rights of our constitution guarantees protection of human rights. Violation of these rights can be protected by issuing writs under article 32 and under article 226 of the Indian constitution in the Supreme Court and High Courts. [4]

'Democratic Republic' stands for the good of all people is embodied in the concept of a 'welfare state' which inspires the directive principles of state policy. The economic justice assumed by the preamble can hardly be achieved if the democracy envisaged by the constitution were confined to a 'political democracy'. In the words of the Pandit Nehru 'democracy has been spoken of chiefly in the past, as political democracy, roughly represented by every person having a vote. But a vote by itself does not represent very much to a person who is down and out, to a person. Let us say, who is starving or hungry. Political democracy by itself is not enough except that it may be used to obtain a gradually increasing measure of economic democracy, equality and the spread of good things of life to others and removal of gross inequalities."[5]

India is a country replete with mutually reinforcing inequalities. Economic inequalities are huge – people die of starvation and live as bonded labours in some regions of the country-while others enjoy an extremely affluent "middle class" lifestyle. Around 300 million of India's one billion population live below the poverty line. Economic inequality means unequal access to health, education and other facilities but it also means unequal access to justice.

Inquality in Economy and Society

Economic inequalities are exacerbated by social inequalities. The existence of the caste system condemns large section of the population to live with little hope of improving their living and employment standards and in fear of atrocities by dominant castes. For tribal people of northeast there is wide spread alienation from a society which is increasingly encroaching on the land and resources on which they rely. In response to the economic development, 'liberalisation' of the economy and globatisation in recent years which have tended to merely exacerbate these inequalities, people's movement have emerged to challenge these forces which threaten the human rights of the vulnerable. The fight against inequality and discrimination at the grass-roots in India growing, fuelled by access to information and increased awareness of rights through the work of activists. Movements within the country have also found support from international initiatives.

Poor people who wonder about, find no work, no wages and starve whose lives are a continual round of sore affliction and pinching poverty, can not be proud of the constitution or its 'law', remarked Dr. Radhakrishnan.

In short, the Indian constitution promises not only political but also social democracy as explained by Dr. Ambedkar in his concluding speech in the Constituent Assembly, "political democracy can not last unless there lies at the base of it social democracy, what does social democracy mean? It means a way of life, which recognizes liberty, equality and fraternity, which are not be treated as separate items in a trinity. They form a union of trinity in the sense that to divorce one from the other is to defeat the very purpose democracy. Liberty cannot be divorced from equality; equality can not be divorced from liberty. Nor can liberty and equality be divorced from fraternity".[6]

The alleviation of poverty, not by expropriation of those who have, but by the multiplication of the natural wealth and resources and an equitable distribution there of amongst all who contribute towards its protection, is the aim of the state envisaged by the directive principles. Economic democracy will be installed in our sub-continents to the extent that minimum needs of all section of the society be achieved and all can strive for a common goal. The economic justice aims at building the economic democracy and if all the resources of a state equally shared by all section of tribal society in northeast- that jurisprudence we might call the state – a welfare state.

Means of Democracy

Democracy in higher sense cannot be established if the minimum rights, for instance, free and civilized existences are not assured to every member of the community. Claiming the protection of human rights is meaningless unless the individuals in a state assured of equality of status and opportunity for the development of the best in him and the means for the enforcement of the rights guaranteed to him.

In the provision of the Indian Constitution it has clearly mentioned that by making illegal all discrimination by the state between one citizen and other citizen, simply on the ground of religion, race caste, sex, or place of birth [Art-15]; by throughing open 'Public places' to all citizens [Art-15 (2)] ; by abolishing untouchability [Art-17]; by abolishing trites of honour [Art-18]; by offering equality of opportunity in matters relating to employment under the state [Art-16]; by guaranteeing equality before the law and equal protection of the laws, as justifiable rights [Art-14]. Article 326 of the constitution refers to the political equality on the ground of providing universal adult franchisee and Article 325 offers the franchisee rights in the elections. This provision has made it mandatory that no person shall be excluded from the general electoral roll allowed to be included in any general or special electoral roll, only on the ground of his religion, race, caste, or sex.

The Universal Declaration of Human Rights says that all people are born equal, so that gives us a new kind of hopes to work, and our governments are also signatory to all these conventions and treaties that talk about human rights so, we want our government to be first responsible and for that human rights activists all over the world, the defenders, the government outside India,[7] the UN should respond to a matter like this (discrimination against minor tribal population), because, the whole matter of conflict is being treated as an internal issue, as a local problem, there are laws and legislation to curb the such discrimination, but in real sense the people are not free in northeast tribal society.

Article 1(3) of the UN Declaration on the Elimination of All Forms of Intolerance and on Discrimination based on religion or belief (1981) states: freedom to manifest one's religion or belief may be subject only to such as are prescribed by law and are necessary to protect public safety, order health or morals or the fundamental rights and freedom of others. The attitude towards human rights activity based on religious discrimination which ignores the fundamental principles on which the UDHR was based – that all human rights should be guaranteed to all, regardless of their religion. Article 18 of the UDHR states: Everyone has the right to freedom of thought, conscience and religion" – has led to attacks on several members of religious minority communities.

Political and Social Discrimination Against Minority

Minorities – the tribes of northeast have got the special status in the Constitution. The Indian Constitution from the very outset abolished any sorts of political and social discrimination against minorities. In the constitution it has been consecrated by the ideas of equality and justice both in the social and political fields, abolishes any discrimination either against or in favour of any class of persons on the ground of religion, race or birth. Our constitution, therefore, prescribes certain measures to help the backward sections to keep up to the same level with the rest of the nation, as well as certain permanent safeguards for the protection of the cultural, linguistic and similar rights of any section of the community, who might be said to constitute a 'minority' from the numerical, not communal, point of view, in order to prevent the democratic machine from being used as an engine of oppression by the numerical majority.

In article 350A, the constitution directs every state to provide adequate facilities for instruction in the mother-tongue at the primary stage of education to children belonging to linguistic minority groups and empowered the President to issue proper direction to any state in this behalf. However, parliament had enacted the National Commission for Minorities Act, 1992 for monitoring the interest of the minority rights under the provisions of the Constitution and state laws.

There are very few places where the people themselves have been able to exercise the power granted by the law, however, it is found that in every place where people are allowed to look after own affairs, in the society. Like in the northeast, it is very necessary to protect the integrity of tribal tradition and culture, and ensure them at least the basic facility by removing all the impediments created by the local state governments, MPs and MLAs and other vested interested parties who do not bother about the rights of the minority religious groups. The state governments must provide the power at their grass root level, and self-rule is the only reality.

In northeast, most of the tribal groups are interested to decide their future in a system of self-rule and that has been seized by the majority population. This is a genuine problem with all the northeastern states. As a result, it is only the majority people exercise the power, not by minority, which leads to regular deprivation against minority tribes of northeast.

What is necessary now is to have a countrywide movement amongst the common people, the deprived minority, to insist that they will strive for the improvement of their lot and that they must have the necessary power under the law, which would enable them to work for their own progress. To promote the spirit of self-reliance mutual cooperation among the people is, therefore, the main task of non-government organisations (NGOs), like radical humanists,

Socialists, progressive Gandhian and a!l those who are willing to work with the people and not merely the people.[8]

There is an incredible sense of alienation and serve incredible on the part of the government to deliver goods and services to people. Today, there is even only a very poor understanding of the needs of mountain people.[9] In the continuous deprivation and discrimination, the minority tribal groups of northeast have become psychologically alienated from its own state. The constitution makers had very positively adhered to the complexity of tribal society and its multiple religious groups.

In the Articles 244, 244 A and part XX1 – consisting of articles 369 to 392 – provided for special status to many states including Nagaland, Mizoram, Sikkim, Arunachal Pradesh, Assam, Manipur and Jammu and Kashmir. In the article of the constitution, the sixth schedule [Article 244(2) and 275 (1)] is concerned with the special arrangements for some kind of "self governance" or so-called the autonomous council of tribal areas in Assam, Meghalaya, Tripura and Mizoram. The central government recognized (Meghalaya) Act 1969 or the Northeast Areas (Reorganisation) Act, 1971 or converted union territories into full fledged states. Until recently Assam government agreed to set up a Bodoland Territorial Council to meet Bodo demands. Every ethnic group has a grievance and the feeling persists, despite constitutional safeguards, that the diverse cultural groups of the northeast are deprived of their legitimate right to govern themselves.[10] India can make a special arrangement of "Self governance" for northeast separately to meet the various needs and demands of the northeastern tribal groups.

The autonomy for Jammu and Kashmir has been made with the special constitutional arrangement provided by the article 370 and same was also made for the Nagaland with the Article 370 A. Experts suggest that the cultural autonomy can be guaranteed under the constitution for multiple ethnic groups, but the administration of the northeast should give the responsibility of a council of elders elected by all major ethnic groups of north-east. The state government shall transfer the powers to the councils, which are with the district and village council and all subjects with regard to the 73rd and 74th constitution amendments on Panchyati Raj and the municipalities.

The financial resources for the council of elders will come from the consolidated fund of India and it will have the power to preserve, protect, initiate changes, lobby for and represent the cultural rights of various communities. It may press for changes at the regional and national levels, in terms of the constitution and the local set-up. It is believed that such an arrangement will protect the integrity of the northeast tribal society and their rights can be safeguarded with out any external interference or can be made them free from the political influence of central and state government. Creating of such 'self-governance' can only be the new form of tribal aspirations is achieved.

NOTES

1. Role of judiciary, PIL and media, p. 33 IIHR.
2. Address to the nation by President Shri K.R. Narayanan of India on the eve of Republic day –2000.
3. *Dr. Shyambhadra Medhi, President, Assam Institute of Sustainable Development,* Parliament and Human Rights, *PRP Journal of Human Rights*, October-December, 2002 ,Pg-23-31,
4. Human Rights at a Glance, *PRP Journal of Human Rights*, October-December,02 Anuran Chakma, Advocate, New Delhi .Pg- 38-39
5. Inaugural address of Pundit Nehru at the seminar on Parliament Democracy on 25-2-1956.The philosophy of constitution, chapter-3,pg-24, D.D.Basu, Wadhwa & Company, 18th edition.
6. Speech of Vice president, *ibid*, The philosophy of constitution, chapter-3,pg- 24, D.D.Basu, Wadhwa & Company 18th edition.
7. Dalit Human Rights Defender Ruth Manorama speaking about the national campaign on Dalit H. Rights at Summit for H. Rights defenders held in Paris Dec.1998.
8. V.M. Tarkunde, Senior Advocate, Supreme court, Need for People Power, *The Statesmen*, 27 October, 2002.
9. Professor P.Lama, Lama of Many Hats,JNU, *The Times of India*. October, 21, 2002.
10. C.P. Bhambhri, former dean of department of social sciences, JNU, One Country two System,New Delhi, *The Statesmen* report, July, 13,2002.

9 Expert Observation and International Recommendation

Expert observation, international recommendations and suggestions on IDP problem in Northeast

[IDPs in the Northeast said to live under inhuman conditions,2000-2001]

Government policies toward indigenous peoples that have become displaced as a result of armed conflict claimed to be inadequate throughout the northeast, conditions for the displaced are poor and no intergovernmental or international organisations are present.

Food aid arrives sporadically and is insufficient IDP camps in both Assam and Tripura reportedly lack of clean water, proper sanitation, mosquito nets, clothing, proper shelters and access to education. "Government policies toward indigenous peoples that have become displaced as a result of armed conflict, though sometimes well intentioned, have been woefully inadequate. Since the early 1990s, hundreds of thousands of people have been displaced in the northeast and Kashmir. However, the government has yet to develop a coherent IDP policy.

IDPs in the northeast remain vulnerable to infectious disease, malnutrition, and rebel attacks. Thousands of Reangs have died in starvation and disease, and 32 people were killed in a 1997 attack on a relief camp in Tripura State. Although hundreds of Kashmiri Hindus must reside in cardboard "rooms" in displacement facilities in Delhi,

Kashmiri IDPs overall have received more substantial rehabilitation packages than their northeastern counterparts, including semi-permanent housing and educational and medical facilities."[1] Although the Kashmiri Pandits in general receive more assistance than internally displaced in the northeast, the camp conditions are criticized: "The Pandit community criticizes bleak physical, educational, and economic conditions in the camps and fears that a negotiated solution giving greater autonomy to the Muslim majority might threaten its own survival in Jammu and Kashmir as a culturally and historically distinctive group." [2]

There are several reports that the conditions for displaced in the Northeast are poor:

> "Throughout the northeast, conditions for the displaced are poor. Violence and displacement continue in some areas, and no intergovernmental or international organisations are present. Many of the displaced live in public buildings and makeshift shelters. Most receive little medical care and have no access to formal education. Many receive food aid, but it often arrives sporadically and is insufficient." [3]

Conditions in IDP Camps in Assam

Over 200,000 IDPs now live in 78 relief camps in Kokrajhar and Bongaigaon districts of Assam. Conditions are very poor. Shelters consist of rows of temporary sheds made of polythene and aluminium sheets. People sleep on the ground on makeshift beds of bamboo; and there is a lack of clean drinking water; and diseases such as malaria, jaundice, dysentery, diarrhoea and influenza pose a serious threat. Groups of five to six people are forced to share essentials. To supplement food rations, which are adequate for at most 10 days a month, they are compelled to consume snails, insects and wild plants. Pregnant women, children, and the elderly suffer the highest health risks in the camps. Over the past couple years, camps have been attacked repeatedly, leaving several dead and dozens injured.

Conditions in IDP camps in Tripura

"The 36,000 displaced Reangs in Tripura live in a camp in Kanchanpur in conditions that Prof. K. Debbarma of Shillong

University calls 'inhuman'. They lack proper sanitation, mosquito nets, and clothing, and their shelters do not have proper roofs. There is no supply of clean drinking water in the camp. According to Debbarama, the displaced take water from streams that are unclean. He said that hundreds of people have become ill or died from dysentery. Doctors from a local hospital visit the camp but lack sufficient medications. The displaced in Tripura are receiving some food aid; some also find day labor. That is causing tensions with poor local people, however, as the displaced often work for lower wages. Locals are also upset because the displaced are cutting much firewood and causing deforestation.

On December 25, 1997, *The Hindu* reported that 17 displaced Reangs in Tripura had died between November 3 and December 16 of starvation and disease. It said, "The situation (in the camps) took a turn for the worse after the state government suspended supply of rations on December 1, putting pressure on the refugees to return to their state." Further health problems were reported in mid-1998.

According to the *Statesman* report published on June 6, 1998 "More than 100 Reang refugees have succumbed to gastroenteritis in camps in north Tripura over the last fortnight." [4]

"UN Guiding Principle 18 (on Internal Displacement) talks about making available essential food, potable water, basic shelter, essential medical services, etc. The conditions in the camps are not satisfactory as they lack basic amenities. There is no facility for education. The central government is meeting the expenditure in providing assistance in terms of essential food and other amenities but the same is not adequate enough considering their long stay in camps.

The state government of Tripura is also not able to provide adequate assistance as the state is currently afflicted with serious insurgency problems and ethnic conflicts. As the Reangs are not getting adequate assistance, Principle 18 stands violated to some extent." [5]

"In Mizoram fearing persecution from the ethnic majority Mizos, 15,000 to 50,000 Reang tribals have fled their homes since 1997 and found shelter in north Tripura, border villages of Assam and the

Chittagong Hill Tracts of Bangladesh. In order to accelerate the repatriation process, the Tripura government discontinued food rations and medical services in some camps, causing at least 16 people to starve to death. At least 260 IDPs died as a result of inadequate shelter and unclean water, and around 1,400 reportedly became seriously ill. Additionally, displacement camps are susceptible to attacks and mismanagement, for which the National Human Rights Commission castigated the Mizoram government in a 1998 report.

Responsibility of the Government

It is clear that the government of India must do more to protect the fundamental rights to life, security and dignity of the IDPs. Not only is current ass'stance and protection inadequate, government policy towards IDPs is inequitable, with Kashmiri Pandits receiving more assistance than their tribal northeastern counterparts.

Additionally, through the reduction of food rations and medical assistance, the government ignobly pressures IDPs to return to areas in which they feel unsafe.

To redress these problems the government needs to develop a strong legal and institutional framework. The Guiding Principles on Internal Displacement, submitted to the UN Commission on Human Rights in 1998, provide a sound ethical and pragmatic foundation for such a framework for IDPs. Drawing heavily from existing international treaties and conventions, the Guiding Principles include the rights of IDPs to assistance and protection without discrimination. The Constitution of India also affirms basic rights to life, food, and shelter. Together, these legal obligations can help structure a workable solution to these problems.[6]

The government should also strengthen its institutional capacity to assist IDPs by enhancing communication between vulnerable populations, their state governments and the central government. Displaced women, as household managers, must be involved in decision-making and assistance distribution to IDPs. Existing channels between displaced groups, administrations and security forces must be made more transparent in order to improve protection and prevent army abuses such as rape, arbitrary arrest and murder.

Finally, assistance and protection for IDPs in India must be supplemented by the vision and political will to bring lasting peace to the northeast. Causes of conflict should also be addressed along with the symptoms of conflict such as internal displacement.

Future wars and internal conflict are likely to produce more IDPs than official refugees. In addressing the plight of IDPs in the northeast it was mentioned, India can become an important frontrunner for future international law and policy developments.

The federal government in India has so far discouraged foreign NGOs or multilateral organisations like the UNHCR from intervening even in standard refugee situations, let alone on internal displacement issues. The UNHCR was kept away from the camps sheltering nearly sixty thousand Chakma and other tribal refugees, who had fled into the northeast Indian state of Tripura from Bangladesh's Chittagong Hill Tracts. For eleven years, the UNHCR was not allowed anywhere near the camps in Tripura because (a) India believed in a bilateral solution of the refugee problem with Bangladesh (b) the UNHCR intervention was seen as capable of internationalising the Chittagong Hill Tracts issue and would have adversely reflected on India's not-so-well-known backing to the PCJSS and its armed wing, the Shanti Bahini (c) Delhi was uncomfortable in letting UN organisations into the northeast, an area where entry of foreigners, even tourists, was almost totally barred until recently, and where such entry is still quite restricted in the four states.

Some experts wonder, though, whether the federal government or the Tripura government would welcome the UNHCR to the Reang camps. Where two state governments are not involved and the displacement has largely taken place within a state, like in Manipur, the chances of UNHCR being allowed to handle an internal displacement situation seems remote at least for the moment. The UNHCR or similar organisations need to evolve a strategy to negotiate access, and enforce the *Guiding Principles* and provide critical humanitarian assistance to beleaguered communities, when the situation demands. Belatedly some state governments, who resent receiving heavy IDP flows, have welcomed foreign NGOs and might be welcoming UNHCR and other UN bodies". [7]

Professor Memon remarked that there is no national legislation on displaced persons, but the existing legal framework should provide sufficient protection and assistance. He mentioned several judicial tools making up this framework. Most importantly, IDP, as citizens of India, should be protected under constitution of India. Secondly, internal treaties such as citizens of India the Universal Declaration of Human Rights, the Convention on the Rights of the Child and the Convention of the Elementary of All Forms of Discrimination against Women, together with national judicial decisions, make up part of India jurisprudence and are applicable in India.[8]

Prevention and Protection from Displacement

In theory the Indian Constitution and other legal safeguard protect citizens from displacement. However, not enough is done to prevent violations of these legal provisions. It stressed the need for both the national government and state governments to address the causes of displacement: competition for territories and economic and political power, leading to religious and ethnic tensions and on the other hand development projects that are not in public interests.

It was suggested that the authorities should pay more attention to conflict to prevent displacement. In that context, it was considered important that local and national authorities refrain from favouring one or another ethnic group for political purposes.

The displaced population often flee due to violation of human rights or threats to their safety but often there are explicit orders to leave, issued by the opposing religious or ethnic group.[9] Experts reported that in northeastern states, so called 'quit notices' were commonly circulated to force one particular group to leave the area. It is noted that IDP's right to life and physical integrity was often violated, even in the camps. Sudden attacks have created a feeling of vulnerability and insecurity among the displaced, even in the camps.

Several cases of discrimination against displaced communities were brought to the notices. Most commonly one group of citizens discriminate against another, but sometimes even the authorities take side in the inter-ethnic or inter-communal dispute and violate citizens' right to non-discrimination.[10] For instance, Reangs were settled in Tripura for more than six years but Mizoram government denies them the access of living in the state, in spite of their rights to live in Mizoram against the direction of the NHRC and courts of India.

The problem of Chakmas in Arumachal Pradesh and Bodos vs Santals can be cited very emphatically. State government has openly discriminated Chakmas by not providing social services, not proceeding their applications for citizenship. It was different even in the case of Santals how they were discriminated by Bodos and state government. It was observed that during their shelter in the camps most funds seem to go to the Bodo community.

In order to improve IDPs' access to social services and to guarantee constitutional rights, experts saw a greater need for issuance of personal identity documents. The situations in a number of IDP camps in the northeast were considered very critical. They believe that Reangs displaced from the state of Mizoram to the state of Tripura had not been properly attended to or received support to return. It was reported that Reangs in the camp in Kanchanpur(Tripura) live under deplorable and life threatening conditions, which has led to number of deaths from curable diseases. Some participants argued that the insufficient camp support from the Tripura state government is a deliberate strategy to force them to go back to Mizoram state.

Many were upset that Medicines Sans Frontiers- Holland (MSF), currently operating in neighboring Assam, were denied state government permission to provide health care in the critical Reang camps in Tripura. There were large number of children have died from very basic diseases.[11] It was suggested that state governments should invite international agencies and the displaced should participate in the dialogue of the humanitarian needs.

The security threats in northeast are also an important obstacle to the return of Reang refugees, but experts believe that the state governments can address them. The return of Reangs from Mizoram, currently in camps in Tripura state, has been ordered by Central government and the Indian Human Rights Commission. Some experts monitoring the situation on Reang repatriation have stressed the need to eliminate discrimination against returning or resettling populations by involving host communities, local authorities and the displaced in the design of return or resettlement plans. Such plans need to take into consideration region specificities, traditions and culture.

Resettlement and rehabilitation of victims of development is a controversial and technically complex issue. Cash compensation has often been given but livelihoods have not been restored. Experts felt that Indian authorities should urgently address the root causes of these ethnic conflicts. It was said that the UN could do little to address the root causes, but the guiding principles could be useful as a moral yardstick to measure the performance of the actors.[12]

Legal and Treaties Division of the Ministry of External Affairs welcomed the efforts to have the guiding principles accepted as normative framework but also adhered to the facts that the rights restated in the IDP guiding principles are also covered by the Indian Constitution and that there are Courts and Procedures in place to address the rights of the displaced. The guiding principles had been too focused on the rights and obligations and that not enough had been included on the national sovereignty. Sufficient allocation of resources as an obligation under international human rights, but called for a sense of realism when looking for solutions of the plight of displaced persons. It stressed the need to objectively look at each such offer and decide on a case-by-case basis.

Causes and Background of Displacement

Although India has been prone to violence it has generated few refugees. However, war, conflict, human rights abuses and forced relocation have created a high level of internal displacement. Estimating the number of IDPs in India is problematic. Regular monitoring is not possible in such a huge country which lacks a central authority responsible for coordinating data from central and state governments.

The nature, frequency and extent of the causes of internal displacement in India are so varying that it would be a herculean task to monitor and record them. Political sensitivities at state level prevent release of data on the exact nature and extent of displacement.

There is thus huge variation in estimates of the numbers of IDPs in India. The latest *World Refugee Survey* put the total number of IDPs in India as 507,000; the Indian Social Institute in Delhi places it at 21.3 million (mainly development-induced displacement); and the Global DIP Project places it at 3.9 million (conflict-induced internal displacement).

The majority of cases in which people have been forced to flee their homes are the consequence of government pursuit of political goals and development objectives. Development-induced displacement has overwhelmingly dominated the IDP scenario in India. Alongside development-induced displacement new causal factors are fast emerging. Unlike the global scenario in the cold war days where population displacements were most frequently caused by armed conflicts fuelled by big power rivalry, in South Asia the so-called post-cold war 'destructured conflicts' or 'low intensity wars' have generated displacement for a long time. [13]

In India there are four categories of internal displacement.

I. Political causes, including secessionist movements

i) Since independence, north-east India has witnessed two major armed conflicts – the Naga movement primarily led by the National Socialist Council of Nagaland, and the Assam movement led by the All Assam Students Union and now largely taken over by the extremist United Liberation Front of Assam. The violence and retaliatory responses from the government and other forces opposed to the secessionists continue to generate a steady flow of displaced people.

ii) In Kashmir's 'war' between state forces and militants, the killing of Kashmiri Pandits by fundamentalist secessionist groups, the widespread anarchy created by political instability and the continuous violation of fundamental human rights by both the state and militant groups, have led to large scale displacement, mainly of Kashmiri Pandits (estimated at 250,000), to Jammu and cities like Delhi. Despite the election and restoration of a popular government in 1996, those displaced have not been able to return due to the continuing reality of sporadic massacres in Kashmir. Although conditions are miserable, the displaced find that camps offer better employment opportunities, education and security.

II. Identity-based autonomy movements

Identity-based autonomy movements, such as in Bodoland, Punjab, Gorkhaland and Ladakh, have also led to violence and displacement. This has happened in Punjab and more recently in the Bodo Autonomous Council area of western Assam. 'Cleansing' of non-Bodo communities by the Bodos, through plunder, arson, massacre and persecution, has forced a large number of non-Bodos to flee. They now live in camps.

III. Localized violence

Internal displacement has also arisen from caste disputes (as in Bihar and Uttar Pradesh), religious fundamentalism (as in urban riots in Bombay, Coimbatore, Bhagalpur and Aligarh) and aggressive denial of residency and employment rights to non-indigenous groups by supporters of the 'son-of-the soil policy' (as in Meghalaya by the Khasi students and in Arunachal Pradesh against the Chakmas).

IV. Environmental and development-induced displacement

In order to achieve rapid economic growth, India has invested in industrial projects, dams, roads, mines, power plants and new cities which have been made possible only through massive acquisition of land and subsequent displacement of people. According to the figures provided by the Indian Social Institute, the 21.3 million development-induced IDPs include those displaced by dams (16.4 million), mines (2.55 million), industrial development (1.25 million) and wild life sanctuaries and national parks (0.6 million). [14] Internal displacement resulting from political and communal violence exists in two main regions of India: the Northeast and Kashmir. The international community is cognizant of the displacement from Kashmir, the result of a long-standing conflict between the Indian armed forces and separatists among Kashmir's Muslim majority that has led to clashes between India and Pakistan. Various Indian and international groups monitor and report on the situation of the mostly Hindu displaced Kashmiris, and the Indian authorities assist them. But the displacement in northeast India has gone virtually unnoticed. The international community, and even many within India, know almost nothing of the scale and nature of the displacement, its causes, conditions for the displaced, or the response of the national or local authorities.

In recent years, tension between the Hindu majority and the Muslim and Sikh minorities in India has escalated, encouraged by political party rivalries and growing Hindu nationalism. In 1990, Hindus destroyed a Muslim mosque in Ayodhya that they claimed was built on the site of an ancient Hindu temple. Subsequent Hindu-

Muslim clashes across India left 1,200 dead. Tension between different Hindu castes could also result in conflict and displacement. In June 1999, some 200 Dalits became displaced in Tamil Nadu State when upper caste Hindus attacked them. The Dalits, long-exploited members of a lower Hindu caste, sought to use public property in their village from which upper caste Hindus traditionally barred them. Further outbreaks of communal violence in densely populated India, which now has one billion inhabitants, could result in massive internal displacement. How India responds to its current displaced populations might be an indicator of how it would respond to major displacement in the future." [15]

India has no national policy and legal institutional framework to deal with either refugees or IDPs. India has not ratified the 1951 Convention and 1967 Protocol and does not permit UNHCR access to most refugee groups. In the absence of a permanent institutional structure to oversee refugee issues, the granting of refugee status has been at the discretion of the political authorities. Due to a similar absence of a national policy on resettlement and rehabilitation of IDPs, there has been only piecemeal and *ad hoc* initiatives at project and state level. Even the latest Draft National Policy for Rehabilitation of Persons: Displaced as a Consequence of Acquisition of Land proposed by the Ministry of Rural Development does not deal with any other type of displacement except that arising from land acquisition. This draft also totally disregards the plight and interests of IDPs of other categories, including those fleeing human rights violations, physical violence and communal and other sources of tension.

Crucially, government accountability for the consequences of state-imposed displacement has been virtually absent. While the states have aggressively clamoured for more benefits from development projects, they have consistently haggled over their share of rehabilitation costs and totally disregarded the plight of those displaced. The draft of National Policy for Rehabilitation is a multi-dimensional response to displacement with full rehabilitation covering i) the entire community (landless labourers, landholders, houseless, householders and even the unemployed and the forest dwellers), ii) their socio-cultural cost of displacement and iii) economic dimensions such as upgrading of skill levels and the accumulation of physical assets as well as social capital. The draft, however, is still under consideration in Parliament.

There is no international agency to deal with such types of displacement. UNHCR's mandate in this regard has been both *ad hoc* and unsystematic. Only recently has UNHCR redefined its mandate to allow for the inclusion of IDPs in certain situations; when such people are present in or going back to the same areas as returning refugees; when they are living alongside a refugee population and have similar needs for protection and assistance; where the same factors have given rise to both internal and external population movements and where there are good reasons for addressing those problems by means of a single humanitarian operation; where there is a potential for cross-border movement and where the provision of assistance to the internally displaced may enable them to remain in safety in their own country.

Future Scenario

As Lama averred, "there seems to be no immediate solution to IDP issues in India. Among other reasons this could be attributed to i) the intricacies and complexities involved in the situations under which they are forced to leave their homes, ii) the low priority given by both the central and the state governments to IDP/refugee issues and the withdrawal syndrome shown by civil society and other interest and pressure groups and iii) the absence of clear-cut policy and national legal instruments and institutions to deal with both pre- and post - displacement situations. Unless the Indian government seriously considers various measures to deal with the causes, displacement may increase and become even more complex.

State responsibility is paramount. Measures must be taken to:

- reduce the level of violence against non-combatants, irrespective of the nature of the conflict
- deal with potential and ongoing ethnic conflicts
- minimize non-ethnic civil conflicts
- avoid repressive measures and ensure that measures and international action are preventive rather than ameliorative

- consider development projects in the larger perspective of sustainable development and human needs
- ensure rapid resettlement and rehabilitation of displaced people
- implement national laws and policies to deal with the multi-dimensional character of IDP groups. [16]

NOTES

1. South Asia Human Rights Documentation Centre (SAHRDC), 16 March 2001, No Refuge: the Plight of Conflict-Induced Internally Displaced Persons in India, [Internet].
2. U.S.DOS, February 2001, Section 5.
3. U.S. Committee for Refugees (USCR), June 2001, *World Refugee Survey 2001* [Internet].
4. Northeast India's Hidden Displacement, U.S. Committee for Refugees (USCR), 2000.
5. K.C.Saha, UN Guiding Principles on Internal Displacements: A Case Study of Internally Displaced Reangs of Mizoram in North-Estern India, (2000 p.11)2000, [Views expressed in this paper are the author's personal views and not the view of the Government of India.]
6. Human Rights Features. (Voice of the Asia-Pacific Human Rights Network) (A joint initiative of SAHRDC and HRDC).
7. *Subir Bhaumik*, Negotiating Access: Northeast India, Paper presented at the Regional Conference on Internal Displacement in Asia. 22 February 2000.
8. Global IDP project, Training workshops on The UN Guiding Principles on Internal Displacement, *India repor*t, 28-30- November, 2001; P-2.
9. Protection from and during displacement, Global IDP project, Training workshops on The UN guiding Principles on Internal Displacement, India report, 28-30- November, 2001, P- 5.
10. Recruitment of minors and forced recruitment, Global IDP project, Training workshops on The UN Guiding Principles on Internal Displacement, India report, 28-30- November, 2001. P- 6.
11. Humanitarian assistance, Global IDP project, Training workshops on The UN Guiding Principles on Internal Displacement, India report, 28-30- November 2001. P- 7.
12. Conflict-induced displacement in the Northeast, Training workshops on The UN Guiding Principles on Internal Displacement, India report, 28-30- November 2001. P- 9.

13. Mahendra P Lama, Internal displacement in India: causes, protection and dilemmas. FMR 8 August 2000.

14. Mahendra P Lama, Internal displacement in India: causes, protection and dilemmas, in Forced Migration Review. *Review of the University of Oxford/Norwegian Refugee Council*, August 2000, p.24-25. [Internet]

15. *Northeast India's Hidden Displacement*, U.S. Committee for Refugees (USCR, p-1), 2000,

16. Mahendra P Lama, Associate Professor at the School of International Studies, Jawaharlal Nehru University, New Delhi.

10 Democracy, Culture and Language Affinity in the North-East

It is difficult to epitomize the disputes without having a sense of common political identity among the tribal people of northeast. Without which it is difficult for them to sustain. This identity may be derived from a shared historical experience which transcends the differences of religion, ethnicity, language or whatever. Political institutions that are recognized as treating all groups fairly, and to which they have all freely consented, may also foster it. Nothing fuels communal antagonism more surely than when exclusion from political office brings with it the experience of discrimination; disadvantage or oppression for one or other community or the fear that it will do so short-sighted political leaders may gain temporary advantage by playing on such fears.

However, secession or partition even when they are practicable, tend to be desperate remedies, which simply transfer the problem to a different point, by creating a newly aggressive minority. It is no answer to historical oppression to construct new oppression for the future.

Intermingling and differences among peoples, races and faiths, which are now the usual norm of contemporary northeastern tribal society. The rights of minorities that are pervaded in arrangement of constitution that serves to protect minorities against planned discrimination and oppression. The independence of the country though brought a final solution of the vital political problem the cultural tangle, far from being resolved, seemed to become worse.

The question of the official language, national language, particularly gave the rise to grave differences. It seemed that our national unity instead of growing stronger was in danger of becoming weaker.[1] The language controversy in northeast is in full peril among tribal societies but even it cannot be avoided as it is inevitably linked with their democratic rights.

It was felt necessary and envisaged for the regional languages when representative government was set up in India. The necessary of keeping close contact with the people and for more effective communication with them it was better, if this could be done in their own language. In the obvious implication English was replaced by each regional language in their areas. After a sharp long controversy the language problem seen to have changed, through drawn up by constitution. Each state was given the power to adopt any language for its official business.

To give further impetus to the regional languages, provisions were made in the constitution about the official language of the union and state governments had made useful suggestions about implementing them. The language flourishment in India has given a wider scope to all major regional languages to provide a social integration, within their own sphere and to build a regional culture. But in the construction of regional prosperity, it has further ripened into greater trouble.

Many tribal groups in northeast have now started demanding their own cultural prosperity, language identity and its reorganisation. Most of the tribal groups, who are fighting for their democratic rights, have one thing common in their mind is that without reorganisation of their language their social and political recognisation is not possible. It has been seen that conflicts as such these turn up to communal violence, when government deny recognising the language or any tribal group oppese their demand.

The Decision of Majority is not Always Democratic

It is a common misconception to equate democracy with majority rule. The term democracy literally as is rule by people, which means rule by whole, not by one part of the people over another. Alternatively, in the decision making of establishing the democratic features of a society it should share equally in all sections of the society, either minority or majority. But in northeast society, the majority,in most cases rules the democratic function. There is no point to be argued here that minority should take major rule in the decision making process. The decision of the majority is always seen more democratic than to allowing minority to exercise their decision, obstructing the will of the majority in a state. So, the meaning of a democratic society will be more transparent if minorities are allowed in the key decision making process in a state.

Principle of Reciprocity

Defenders of majority rule point out that those minorities on one occasion may in the majority on the next, and that their lack of influence in one decision, or in one election, will be compensated by winning later. Minority consent to the majority view, in other words, rests upon a norm of reciprocity; then turn to be in majority will come, and others will have to respect it in the same manner as they have done. However, this principle of reciprocity breaks down if the decision impairs a minority's capacity to canvass its views in the future; or if the minority is a 'Permanent' one; or it cannot be compensated by wining on different issues in the future. Each of these cases acquired separate examination.

Minority and Individual Rights

When the majority, or the government acting with majority support (as in case of Mizoram government is acting as per the wishes of Mizo majority) infringes the basic democratic rights of an individual or group (as Reangs). It clearly defines undemocratic. These basics are necessary to enable people to contribute to political life, social right, free cultural expression, free voting powers and rights of citizenship. Freedom of speech, movement empowered all Indian citizens in our constitutional framework or democratic system; ideally they should be given special protection in a constitution or bill of rights, where they remain immune from majority infringement.

Rights of Citizenship in a Democratic Society

In principle the state of right to determine — who may become a member or citizen and how citizenship rights are acquired. But in the exercise of the sovereign power it must not behave in a discriminate way, for example, by operating a racially discriminatory immigration policy or skirting off the names of the authorised and privileges upon those who were entitled to Indian citizenship in India.

It's simply described the classes of persons who would be deemed to be the citizens of India at the date of the regulation by some future law made by parliament. In exercise of this power, parliament has enacted the citizenship Act (57 of 1955), making elaborate provisions for the acquisition and termination of citizenship subsequent to the commencement of the constitution. The various modes of acquisition of citizenship prescribed by the citizenship Act,1955, (a) citizen by birth (b) citizenship by descent (c) citizenship by registration (d) citizenship by naturalization (e) citizenship by incorporation of territories.[2]

In Article 15(1) of the constitution stated that the state should not discriminate against any citizen on grounds of religion, race, cast, sex, place of birth or any of them.[3] It must also abide by any international agreement it has ratified at the admittance of refugees.

Minority Rights in Democracy

International Human Rights norms offer special status for minority communities, whether defined as entitled not only to have the state recognise their existence, but also to have it protect their specific identity and to encourage conditions for the promotion of that identity.

Persons belonging to minorities should have full democratic rights, including the rights to have the equal opportunity in the affairs of the state as also to participate in decisions that affect their particular communities or the regions in which they live.

UN Declaration on Minorities

These and other principles are set out in the Unites Nations. Declaration on the rights of persons belonging to National or Ethnic, Religious and Linguistic minorities adopted by the General Assembly of the United Nations in December 1992. Many if not most states have minority communities, and positive approach to the rights of its minorities.

In the International sphere, the demand for special safeguards to protect the culture or linguistic identity of minority communities has emerged from the principle that owing to war, or like circumstances causing territorial changes without the consent of the people residing in those territories, the identity of such communities who have been torn asunder by circumstances beyond their control should be preserved form ethnic extinction, by affording proper safeguards through international charters and national constitutions. In 1966, the international covenant was adopted and included Article 27 saying that; in those states in which ethnic, religious, or linguistic minorities exist, persons belonging to such minorities shall not be denied the right, in community with the other members shall not be denied the right, in community with the other members of the group to enjoy their own culture, to profess and practice their own religions, or to use their own language. Indian Constitution of 1949 guarantees them as the fundamental rights of the minorities in Article 25, 29, 30.

In international fora, it has been emphatically made clear that the only object of offering minority safeguard was to protect the minority from discrimination by the majority who administer a country or state under a representative system of democracy.

The framers of the Indian constitution believe that, having established a secular state, (i.e. a state which has no established religion of its own, and treats all religion equally) and offers safeguards for the preservation of the religions, culture and linguistic identity of the minorities, not only Muslims, but also all the minorities who remembered in India as citizens, would be united as one national by bond of fraternity.[4]

Language Recoganization

The language recognisation is also a long halting process of their society which has not been allowed them to enjoy the rights to use it officially or in school education. It is once again a long-term barrier in tribal integration of northeast. The dispute within the interrelationship of government and individual tribal group and within the majority and minority has generated from the derecognisation of their language. Most of the separatist groups who are fighting for their democratic rights are also demanding their language recognisation so called the 'language autonomy'. Most of the tribal groups in northeast are fighting a tough battle against the state governments in want of their mother tongue, should be recognized for official use and implement a policy to use the language for tribal education in their areas.

The language recognisation, however, had received immense popularity in various states of India just after India's independence. It had taken to the shape of a popular movement in the whole country. The congress leadership, during that time, did not oppose this popular move. Until 1960, this issue intensified this language movement among all the regional population and most of the political parties seemed to support it following the JVP report. A peculiar shape turned when some linguistic groups moved in the line of recognising the states.

The state recognisation may not help all the time to resolve the problems relating to linguistic conflicts in northeast. The language problem finds a greater space apart from other demands such as autonomy, political, civil and economic rights.

Most of the tribal groups in northeast feel that the recognisation of their mother tongue is the halfway to fulfilling their democratic rights. Individual groups are in a constant move, fighting to add more 'values' in their democratic system and always compare with other rival tribal groups. Granting the 'language dignity', they feel, is a certain status and this will allow them to say that-'ours society have the status and dignity in the state and no one can suppress us.' That is why most of the tribes and non-tribes in erstwhile Assam, opposed to learn the Assamese language as medium of communication and education. After a bid of battle, Bengalis have got their language recognization, now they pursue their education in their mother tongue and others are still waging for the same.

I could remember the strong struggle of "Bishnupriya", who once inhabitabed in Manipur state and now settled at many places of Assam, fighting for the recognisation of their language and to use the word 'Manipuri' for their social recognisation. They attended many beleaguers, strikes and roadblocks. Their language movement claimed many lives. Quite interestingly, they had no any other demand as such, but wanted only their language recognisation, which was refused by the state government of Assam. In the same way, Reangs are also demanding its own official language *'Kakborok'*.

From the very beginning, it was adhered, to decide upon the status and rights of these minorities in the states. On the other hand, there was the question of their protection, there was ever- present danger on them being meted out unfair treatment, on the other there was the need to promote their integration with the major language group of the state. A linguistic minority had to be given the confidence that it would not be discriminated against by the majority and that its language and culture could continue to exist and develop. At the same time, the majority had to be answerable that meeting the needs of the linguistic minority would not generate separate sentiments or demands, and that minorities would develop a degree of state loyalty.[5]

To solve the language problem, Indian constitution made the language provisions. It has provided certain fundamental rights to linguistic minorities such as the Article 30 which facilitates that all minorities whether based on religious or language, shall have the rights to establish and administer education institutions of their choice.

Therefore, the state shall not discriminate any educational institution, if though under the management of minority group, in granting the aids. Article 347 says that the 'President may direct that its language shall be officially recognised throughout the state or any part thereof for such purposes as he might specify. The official policy, since 1956, in a constitutional amendment laid down the necessary instructions for the use of mother tongue, in the primary and secondary classes, whenever the numbers of children are found to be sufficient. A commission for reviewing the linguistic minorities' interest was suggesting to be set up by the constitution. The minority commission in time to time has found the genuine problem of innumerable cases of discrimination against linguistic minorities in the matters of schooling, admission to technical and medical institutions and employment in the state public services because of lack of proficiency in the official language in the state. [5] Though central government has taken a very tentative role for the safeguards of the linguistic minorities and left it upon the state governments to decide the problem of the linguistic minority.

But the policy of central government differs and most of the state governments do not initiate to take the linguistic problem into action. The role of the most of the state governments in northeast was very negative and unsatisfactory. By and large, the governments took no interest to safeguard the interest of the linguistic minorities.

Historical Reasons in Notheast Problem

The then British were also held responsible for the present situation in northeast. In one time British government permitted and encouraged Christian missionaries to take the charge of educating tribesmen and for other community services. The missionaries, in turn, collaborated with colonial authorities and helped keeping the national influence out of the tribal areas, rather than encouraging their isolation from the rest of the population of erstwhile northeast and India. After independence, those missionaries and other foreigners even prompted sentiment in favour of separate and independent states in northeast India.[6]

The virtual difference struck into the society with rest of the country in the long disillusionment of political and cultural conflicts. But the British has brought the Christian missionaries in northeast that generally made of the tribal peoples to feel anti-Indian.

The tribal policy of the government of India insisted by Jawarlal Nehru was the most forwarding step. Since then northeast became the special attention of the central government. On the part of the policy in the sixth schedule of the Constitution it had emphasized for a fare degree of self-governance to the tribal people of northeast in the line of formation of autonomous districts and creation of district and regional councils.

The Constitution even empowered to the councils to excise some of the legislative and judicial functions independently within the auspices of the Assam legislature and the parliament. The six schedule was made in the best way to support tribal societies of northeast to live with their full democratic rights without any external influence from other society or political interference. The provision was made in the constitution to pave the way of tribal autonomy.

The resentment started brewing up in the minds of some tribal groups in the mid-fifties and in the sixties, began to mount up for separate hill state when Assamese political leaders made the Assamese language as sole official language of the state. In 1960, various political parties merged into All Party Leaders Conference (APHLC).

Most of the hill leaders opposed the move of the Assam state government, when they pushed the Assam Official Language Act and ignoring the demand of tribal language in administration, encouraged the tribal groups to carry the movement of separate statehood and tribal autonomy.

Rising Demands for Separate Statehood

On the light of the controversy, several commissions and committee established to examine the northeast situation and finally in 1969 Meghalaya was given the complete statehood autonomy and its law and order remained in the function of the Assam government.

Meghalaya became the full separate state incorporating the other tribes Garo, Khasi and Jaintia tribes. Thereafter union territories of Manipur, Tripura and Arunachal Pradesh were granted statehood. The trouble tickled out in the case of Nagaland and Mizoram, as they were actively involved with insurgency and carried out services of communal disturbances to get their autonomy.[5] On 28 February, 1966 large scale disturbances broke out through Mizoram in which armed Mizo National Front (MNF) forces rose in Mizo rebellion and relentlessly attacked on government officials in Aizal and Lunglei. The then SDO, Lunglei, R.V.Pillai was kidnapped by insurgents. The government treasury at Aizawl was also attacked. The Aizawl bara bazaar was burnt. The MNF were operating from East Pakistan and directing subversive activities in Mizoram and Cachar discricts.

To control the situation, Assam government deployed Military troops and IAF jet aircrafts. In the hostile activities resulting in various attacks on Aizawl, causing deaths and injuries to several persons. Mizoram became the Union on 21 January 1992.But MNF rebels continued their attacks on high ranking officers .The Inspector General and Deputy Inspector General were killed by the rebels in a most shocking manner.

In February 1976, MNF Chief Laldenga signed an agreement after he returned to India from Pakistan. The agreement did not last further, with the coming of Smt. Indira Gandhi to power, the prospects of peace negotiations with the MNF further started. It was declared that government had negotiated with Laldenga and they will suspend all underground activity from the mid-night of 31 July 1980.

The agreement was further failed and hostile activities were as usual. The peace talks resumed again between the government of India and the MNF and both of the participants in peace talks signed the Peace Accord on 30 June 1986. In the Peace Accord it was mentioned that the rights and privileges of the minorities in Mizoram as envisaged in the constitution shall continue to be preserved.

Enough evidence we had from the above statements, that since the very beginning Mizoram was disturbed in insurgency and nefarious activity. Even during the British administration, there had been the conflicting reports and clashes within the inhabited tribes in Mizoram. The history reveals that almost all tribes, including the Mizo majority, migrated from other places and states into Mizoram. The Mara (Mizos call them Lakhers) migrated to Mizoram from the Haka area of the Chittagong Hills Tracks (CHT- Bangladesh) and the Chakmas of Mizoram migrated from the same place.

Mizo Culture and Tradition

According to Mizo traditional belief, the Mizos came from "Chhinling" meaning a covering rock. The Mizo people belonging to various clans came out of the earth from below the stone. In the opinion of the people, Chhinlung is a place called Silung which is situated in China bordering the Shan state of Burma. They migrated later to India via Burma. During the fifteenth century they lived in the hill tracks of Burma, with their main villages located in the valley between the Run and Tiau rivers. The Tiau river is in Burma bordering Mizoram and the Run is further inside Burma.[7] The dominant Mizo tribes were the Lushai which was prosperous.

The society was an egalitarian one, having no particular Chief to rule them. Supremacy among the people belonging to different villages used to be decided by physical fights between the strongest man of one village and that of another. The two would fight hand to hand on the borders of the villages. The village of the winning man would gain command over losing village. The majority Mizos still tend to dominate other minority tribes through the traditional pattern of physical fight and sometime it converts in to gang fights.

The ancestral Mizo society (pre-British era) borne the ample dignity and reputation of equal justice and equal rights for all. The scope of commission of heinous crimes was therefore very limited. Serious crimes like murder, rape and docaity were not prevailing. Mizos are a close-knit society with no class distinction and no discrimination on the ground of sex and religion. Ninety percent of them are cultivators and the village exists like a big family. Birth of a child, marriage in the village is important occasion in which the whole village is involved. The Mizo code of ethics or 'Dharma' moved round 'Tlawmngaihna' an untranslatable term requiring on the part of everyone to be hospitable, kind, unselfish and helpful to others. 'Tlawmngaihna' to a Mizo stands for that compelling moral force which finds expression in self-sacrifice for the service of others.

The Mizo religion before the advent of Christianity was animism. But with invasion of British and Christian missionaries, Mizos have lost their old religion, cultural and identity glory. The multi-cultural society- Mizoram – the living place of many tribals, wherein a search of their identity taken the path of undemocratic steps against the interest of the other tribal society. The way the Mizos have tossed the Reangs out of Mizoram state that was completely against the democratic rights of an individual or society and wrongly directed.

The individual rights could not be achieved through breaching the rights of others or by killing, nabbing or hurting others. Mizoram is inhabited by all migraed tribal groups, Mizos came sooner and others like Chakma, Mara, Lai, Hmar, Reang and Kuki came later. But in a democratic country like India, all of them have got the equal opportunity to live and all of them have the right to citizenship, free exercise of political, economic and religious and such other rights, according to the provision of Indian constitution.

In Mizoram, Maras, Lais and Chakmas were given the status of separate autonomy councils at the time when Mizoram granted the statehood. Reangs are fighting to achieve the similar autonomous status.

In 1961, the census recorded the district population as 2,66,063 of which 2,61,014 were tribes. The tribe wise breakup was – Mizo (Lushai) 2,13,261, Chakma 19,337, Kakher (Mara) 8,790, Pawi (Lai) 4,587, Hmar 3,119 and Kuki including Reang 11,677.

Church Influence in Mizo Society

Rev. William, the first missionary came to Mizoram in 1891 and followed by other two missionaries, J.H. Lorrian and F.W.Savidge, in 1893.They started the first school at Aizawl. Later on many such missionaries arrived at Aizawl such as Re. D.E. Jones and Rev. Edwin Rowland in 1897. The missionaries moved village-to-village spreading the Gospel and providing other social services.

Before 1899, there were no Christians in Mizo society and on the year two young boys Khuma and Khara were baptized becoming the first Christians among the Mizos. Welsh Mission, London Baptist Mission; Lakher Pioneer Mission and some others came in later years such as Salvation Army, the Roman Catholic and the Seventh Day Adventists. All have worked amongst Mizo society. The religious Christianity education now spread almost each and every village in Mizoram.

Over the years of Christian dominance in Mizo society now underwent into total change. The effect of Christianity was observed that the missionaries were destroying some of the customs of the Mizo society. The first impact of Christianity was on the religions beliefs, customs and practices of the Mizos. The new faith dispelled the belief in the multifarious spirits and in the efficiency of appeasement through sacrifices and rituals. Today, Mizoram is coupled with a new Christian culture and has emerged among the Mizos. Despite many efforts to preserve the Mizo identity in high influence of Christian Religion had made many significant changes.

It has even led to delirious effects on the culture, tradition of the Chakma and Reang society, who are the believers of Hindu religion. Non-Christian had the rare chance to get the church services and church education. Many Reangs have denied their religious conversation and hence deprived from the services. But the support and social services of Christian missionaries that actually benefited Mizo people. As a result the literacy rate within Mizo society shot up 36.28 per cent in 1951 from 2.5 per cent in 1901, and now it reached at 88.49 percent (2001).

The existence of Christian Missionaries in Mozoram is now more than one century. Many of the forefront leaders and educated Mizo people brought up through Christian education, carried Christian thoughts and ideology, and even accepted the Christian beliefs, and most of the Mizo people, almost all, converted them into Christianity. In that highly influenced Christian Mizo society, the non-Christian had the rare chance to adjust and equate with them. The leaders of today's generation have been very supportive to missionaries.

The developmental works and government aids that all channelized through them. For this obvious reason and being the non-Christian of Mizoram, Chakmas and Reangs were deprived and discriminated in getting government and other social supports. Since many years and till today, many Reangs have been converted into Christianity, just for getting their fundamental and democratic benefits. Thus many of them survived in Mizoram, who converted them into Christianity and other Reangs who remained as Hindus, have been uprooted from Mizoram. This is the kernel truth and those Reangs now became refugees. Journalists, social writers and researchers do not raise this point, because, it may hurt the religious sentiment. The same point was also echoed by the leaders of refugees in Tripura camps, saying that they could have survived in Mizoram if they sacrificed their religion. But simply they could not sacrifice that.

NOTES

1. Dr. S. Abid Hussain, Towards a new natioal culture, The National Culture of India.
2. Durga Das Basu,Citizenship, chapter-7, *Introduction to the constitution of India,* pp. 73-74.
3. Durga Das Basu, Fundamantal rights and duties, chapter –8, *Introduction to the constitution of India*, p. 90.
4. Durga Das Basu, How the constitution has worked, chapter- 34. *Introduction to the constitution of India*, pp. 412 – 413.
5. Bipin Chandra, Mrudula Mukherjee and Aditya Mukuerjee, *India after Independence*, 1947- 2000, Penguin Books. pp. 103-104
6. Jawarhal Nehru, LM C, Vol 111, p. 150.
7. Mizoram, P. Lalvihanga, Ministry of Infromation & Broadcasting, GOI, 1997. p. 11,12, & 18 .

11 | Conclusion

The Future of Human Rights and Democracy in Northeast

Observing the problems of Reangs and other minorities in northeast which unfold a vast ostracism, clearly denying their minimum rights. Many of those conflicts and violence are taking place in northeast as because of those problems. Terrorist gangs have become the frontrunners, fighting for the rights of minority and deprived people, actively participated in the affairs of killing people in northeastern region. We have seen the case of Reangs in Mizoram, and how they have been driven out of the state. Reangs, the minor tribesmen, don't have minimum democratic rights, as being the citizens of this country.

After Bodo-Santal massacre, perhaps it is rare of its kind in the history of northeast tribal society, – that such a big population, around 52 thousand Reangs, have been uprooted and thronged at different states for shelter. Perhaps, it is also a rare occasion that such large scale violence, killing, torture, gang rape and house burning had been carried out at majority's helm, largely politically vested. These incidences were brought to the notices of human rights agencies and commission to take appropriate action.

What happened with Reang society in Mizoram that was completely unethical and unjustified in modern human society. That clearly unveils government's incapability to protect the interest of minor populace—Reangs. What the majority Mizos had initiated, against Reang villagers, throughout the state, was a pity and shame, discourage human dignity and peaceful living with equal opportunity.

In the growing acrimony of intolerance, discrimination, terrorism, communal clashes, killing innocent people have become the features of these days. In any hostile situation, governments don't step up to prevent such cases and rarely take measures.

Sometime political representatives try to get the maximum benefit when community clashes cripple. Majority Mizos in Mizoram when cleansed the Reangs, the state government (who had the majority Mizo support) and state police were mostly inane in those large-scale violation of human rights. Police were reportedly involved with the Mizo extremists and landed all supports.

The Reangs, largest tribal population in Tripura, have the similar sporadic situation. In Tripura too, they are very poor and backward despite of development activities and innovation of many poor people oriented programmes. State government programmes are only benefiting Bengalis and Tripuris, leaving aside Reangs and other tribal groups.

Population of Assam state face such serious threats from ULFA, NDFB, BLT and many other extremist groups. The All Assam Students Union (AASU), since the inception of Assam movement, has been generating an anti-Bengali and anti-non-Assamese feeling in the state. That Bengalis are Bangladeshis and illegal migrants. Previous government led by Prafulla Kumar Mahanta, who was once the president of AASU, was willing to abolish the IM (DT) Act .It has instigated anti Bengali Hindu and Muslim feeling sometime taken the shape of communal flair up. Earlier, the views propagated by Mahanta, estimating around 70 lakh such foreigners living in the state.

The conflict on Bodo autonomy has given the birth of Bodo Security Force later converted to National Democratic Front of Bodoland (NDFB) killing of 200 innocent people in 1996. Bodo-Santal ethnic clashes that left to over 200,000 people in permanent refugees and many became homeless. The Bodo conflict has further intensified when the then Chief Minister of Assam late Hiteshwar Saikia once assured all the ethnic groups to provide autonomy as per the B.P. Shing recommendations.

But that promise was not fulfilled. Assuming, that was the high political propaganda as a reason of present ethnic crisis in Assam.

The Naga disturbances are unique in having an almost entirely political foundation. But the Naga leaders had an old view that Nagaland was never be a part of India. They wanted a political settlement to minimize the Naga disturbances. Such disturbances were continued for decades.

Discrimination against minority is a common problem with each and every state. Minority tribals in Tripura and Manipur are also fighting for establishing democratic rights. In a nutshell all states are disturbed by such insurgency and ethnic conflicts over to get their fundament rights. Peace no longer exists in all these states. Establishing peace and harmony is a matter of great concern for such religious and culturally diverse states in northeast,while majority population are becoming as the more dynamic force. Following viewpoints may provide a signpost for restoring peace and democracy in northeast.

(1) *Minimizing the Political Inequality and Propagandas*

The degrees of political campaign favouring the majority or certain linguistic groups have to be prevented by making certain norms. Leaders representating various political parties, should maintain a strict adherence of high political norms when they campaign to achieve their agendas or while seeking public support. The wrongly directed political commitment creating an adverse implication on the tribal society and that stimulates the public to attain that commitment.

Sometime aspirant people emotionally involve with the political system. Commitment should be made in accordance to the actual development and guaranteeing the genuine needs of society without any discrimination on the basis of caste and religion or on the basis of minority and majority. The legislators should maintain a pluralistic outlook and create a congenial atmosphere so that all citizens can realise that they have equal opportunity and benifits, and they have equal rights in government resources and services.

Government policies should encourage universal literacy may be more important than to follow the particular level of economic development. And what fledging democracies need more than anything else is sustainable economic growth, from whatever level of development they start, vulnerable sections of a society are able to share in improvement and the intensity of distribution conflicts is moderated.

(2) *Avoid Religious Conflict and Make the Democracy More Powerful*

History repeals us that the religious conflicts (not in all conflicts) have badly affected the development and society both . In the case of Reangs, it is strongly evident that because of their Hindu religion they have been negated and forced to leave their homeland. Other Reangs, who have converted into Christian religion, somehow survived in Mizoram. Forcible religious conversion gives rise to many small and big tensions in northeastern tribal society. It is not even possible to separate the great world faiths by any hard and fast rules. Categories such as those effects are disabling to it, since all religions contain within them a verity of competing tendencies.

Christianity supported both the divine right of kings and egalitarian republicanism. At one and the same time influential groups within this and other faiths have worked to support authoritarian regimes, while other have risked their lives to protect opponents of them, or to expose their human rights violations. The religious authorities regard the state as the devine instrument for fulfilling a religious mission on earth, policies can readily take on the character of a crusader in which members of other faiths are forced into line and persecuted and all freedom of expression becomes stifled.

Any religious missionary should be further taken carefully while using them for the purpose of public services. A watchdog body may can check their activities. Their activity if works for only particular section of the society may be prevented with special norms. Rather time has come to replace the task by NGOs or any neutral institution who do not offer any religious persuasion or conversion.

Religious conversion should not be forced in society. Some religious organisations in northeast involved since decades to offer special safeguard and economic status after conversion. It is a kind of discrimination on the basis of religion when some one offering any services. This has to be changed to minimise the religious discrimination; through overnight it is not possible to change the function of these organisations, but has to be slowly changed with special safeguards.

(3) *Human Rights Cannot Exist in Religious and Ethnic Conflicts.*

Ethnic and religious conflicts arise only when people fail to exercise their democratic rights. That means no common political identity in a state. Conflict arises only when they are approached to live in unequal democratic system. Unequal share of development in government plans and programmes, that clearly makes division within a society. It is common urge to every society that the people within a society can get opportunity to live with certain standards and diginity. While other minority groups have nothing of that sorts that creates a field for fighting. For all these reasons why violence and ethnic conflicts perpetuate in a state.

Political leaders and governments have to be more proactive and responsive to their fellow citizens. Plans and programmes that the leaders offer only on the basis of their long-term existence in government. Such practice in a democratic country is very unfair. Political leaders, sometime offer fabulous programmes and schemes for a particular ethnic group, inviting only political discrimination or oppression against other ethnic groups. Quite frequenty leaders play the cards on religious and ethnic line. Leaders may be gaining temporary benefits but in long run it destructs the society. No doubt the question of enabling the democratic rights is in palpable. But this is not the right way of approaching the citizens in a democratic country. This has to be changed very urgently, through building of basic human rights education within the political circle. Otherwise it will be too late and common citizens will suffer in ethnic conflicts and will face the tranquility of ethnic conflicts.

(4) *Human Rights and Contemporary Conflicts*

They need of the hour is to understand the various aspects of internal conflicts: why it generally turns violent and hostile? The conflicts may be classified into various forms such as: 1) Ideological conflicts between the state and insurgent movements where the social inequality between classes is dominant. 2) Government and authority conflicts concerning the distribution of power and authority in society. Demands for autonomy from the minorty linguistic groups are for control over resources 3) Racial conflicts; discriminating minority and helping the majority in getting jobs, services and other developmental works and 4) Identity conflict: where the dominant aspect is ethnic; religious; tribal; linguistic differences. The identity conflict is one of the key conflicts in northeast increasingly taking a place among tribal groups.

The identity conflicts have subdivided into territorial conflicts, ethnic and minority conflicts, and religious assertions. Largely it has given the shape of terrorism to struggle for self-determination. Identity conflicts are the most pervasive and the most violent. Identification is in inherent and unconscious behavioural imperative in all individuals. Individuals actively seek to identify in order to achieve psychological security and they actively seek to maintain, protect and boldster identity in order to maintain and enhance this. Psychological security, which is a sine qua non of personality, stability and emctional well-being.

Considerable attention has to be given to the tensions between ethnicity and modernisation. Backward and minority classes have that psychological barriers of 'fear to lose'. Quite often they measure themselves with near rivalry groups, and try to justify the achievements, progress and development. In case of any discrepancy in the share of economy and resources, they turn up in mass movement for their democratic rights. Development strategies may have unintended effects on inter ethnic relations. But experts pointed out that development theory must be sensitive to cultural pluralities. This is particularly relevant to development strategies which often ignore minorities and where hegemonic elites and international doner agencies may concentrate only on certain groups. They may shift their attention towards minorities and deprived section of the society.

(5) *Role of the States in Promotion of Human Rights*

States can take the central role in promotion of various ethnic and linguistic groups. Running the government amidst diversified ethnic and cultural groups is a complex task. Government should identify the issues on case to case basis, especially dealing the situation of northeast. The states create and deny the identity of others. Together with the demands of democracy and participation, there are many ethnic and religious minorities demanding greater autonomy, recoganisation and identity. Identifying the problem of minority group and giving a serious thought on it has become the major focus of the governments.

Government responds only when ethnic groups take guns and create violence. This terror-tension is likely to be further compounded by severe poverty and unemployment in the parts of northeastern states. The demand for identity and autonomy will be located within the framework of increasing gaps between the elites and the poor, where their own language, economic freedom and culture may be the final focus of identity in a rapidly changing modernising world to which backward and poor are denied the access.

State and encounter violence serve to exacerbate cleavages. The violation of human rights, including extra judicial killings or torture, has produced a vicious cycle of violence and terror. State violence has brought with it a sense of insecurity; this then acts as a strong force of mobilisation which too often takes extra- parliamentary or militant forms, leading to armed conflicts.

In Reang exacerbated tensions, government had no right policy and largely failed to provide the safety and security. Though the autonomy granted to Chakmas and Maras much before the declaration of Mizo statehood. Even till they have the problem of total control on resources and powers. Full powers have not been granted, still hats off. The Mara Autonomous District Council, which governs the district, members frequently collide each other and tend to split. Alleged that, state government still has the intension to control the council through its nominated members in the council. Recently 23 members executive committee went to court, won their appeal and got the governor to summon a committee meeting on 29 May 2002. But the Mara community of about 60,000 people remains rudderless, under-developed and unhappy. The community people threaten that if government does not solve their trouble, it will prefer to go 'underground' to grab national attention. They also alleged that the majority Mizos have not given them a fair deal and continue to boss over them and that funds to their area ate settled.

The Bodo Autonomous Council in Assam, created in 1993, has been further dismantled into many disputes. Their demand of inclusion of 3085 villages has not granted by the government. The autonomy dispute created severe problem among Santal, Coach and Rajbanshi, and other backward groups of Assam. But constant delay in solving the problem on behalf of the government has racked up anther fresh demand of a separate statehood.

Negotiations do not include the militant group based in Bhutan–National Democratic Front of Bodoland–who seeks independence from India. It is suggested to address key issues; the boundary of the proposed council and reservation seats for the council, assembly and parliament. But this must be seen in a democratic prospective; Bodos are numerical minority in the proposed council. Non-Bodos and non-tribals say, their rights can not be ignored. But to solve the Bodo demands it requires constitutional amendments of the sixth schedule and few relevant articles. Bodoland territories council area has a mixed population and total reservation for tribal rights and governance in the region, now is being extended to the plains.

In Assam, the Karbi Anlong Autonomous Council was created much before in 1950.But that has not provided any democratic rights to the Karbis. It only created few corrupt leaders who misused council grants.No attention was paid to the development of the Karbis. That has lead to the birth of Karbi National volunteers (KNF) in 1995. After merging with KNF another militant group, United People Democratic Solidarity (UPDS) formed in 1999. They all are fighting for their democratic rights. Completing the process of Karbi autonomy, which had promised to dismiss political corruption from the council. Most of the tribal groups are suffering in that disposition in northeast.

When the question comes to tribal autonomy, it is not so difficult to address those tribal issues, logically it depends on the government if allows them to hold their views and gives them an equal opportunity. The whole gamut of the problem can easily be wiped out, if governments' role lies in their incredible performances, and make sure that the needs and demands of minorities are mitigated.

States must not be directed attaining only its limited objectives of capturing political power. But the major objective of a state would be to provide welfare to the minority groups. A credible government try to resolve the most pressing problems of mankind.

People are getting more literate and modern, more aware of their rights and political obligation. Times are not far, the performance of the government, political parties and its leaders will be measured in terms of their success, and in dealing with different situations of complexity of a state.

(6) *Need For a Conflict Management Experts and Human Rights Awareness Program*

The tribal conflict in northeast is swelling so fast than any ancient time. The tribal groups have convinced that bottom line is the self-governance and autonomy.Their demand starts with these and ends with shedding bloods and tears. There is no alternative of violence and terrorism.In recent days there is a growing consensus on the need of preventive action, early warning and prevention of violent conflicts. Government should set up a forum or expert committee to make the debate on early warning and conflict resolution.

A very significant and important instrument in conflict transformation has been the role of elections, national and international monitoring mechanism can be strengthened to facilitate and ensure periodic elections. Such initiatives have been taken recently in Jammu and Kashmir Assembly elections held in the end of the year 2002. As some international experts and independent agencies were active in monitoring the election process.

In a democratic society, the process of restoration of democracy and its proper measures is a good sign. Independent experts may monitor the speeches during the elections, on how political leaders approach the voters to win the election. Is there any propaganda that leaders carry during election that can impede the interest of other community or minority groups. The leaders deliver speeches and promises they made that are beyond their capacity to fulfil. This is to be genuinely vetted and government should set a guideline for the leaders for participating elections.

The level of government corruption is another great problem in northeast. Political leaders and most of the officials within the government are involved in rampant corruptions. Job seeking applicants pay handsome bribes to the political leaders or to higher government authority. No such fare policy was intorduced in development or in distribution of government schemes and services. These sometimes rake up the resentment and insist conflicts.

A monitoring committee should focus on these areas and make sure that the people have not been deprived, not discriminated on the basis of caste, religion, rich or poor. It is a fact that poor people have no access to government jobs, because of their inability to pay high bribes.

So, each problem has some background and reality. Systematic study on the conflict and the findings of the problem can provide valuable insights for making a conflict management strategy. Furthermore, such studies should focus on identification of the actors, domestic conflicts involving groups are often asymmetric or unequal conflicts are not single-issue situations. They inherit a past which acts as a heavy burden on the future. Protected social conflicts involve question and identity, symbolic meaning, control over resources and a sense of meaningful security. More attention has to be paid to conflict transformation. How a framework can be created for conflict resolution. How the terms of reference and the constituency of the conflict can be changed.

(7) *The Model for Resolution of Minority Conflict*

The conflict resolution is the process to continuous holding discussions with the victims group or minority group. The minority conflict is a long dispute of northeast states deeply rooted soon after independence. However, many tribal groups' problems could have been slithered by providing the statehood autonomy. In larger sense, the statehood grant has not given much benefit to the small tribal groups. They remained same to their earlier vulnerable situation.

Within the present system, state governments are unable to uplift the human dignity and the rights of the several tribal groups.Forget about the larger interest of the state people, the leaders, within the government, are more interested to hold the power, indulge high corruption and spend public money for their own welfare. This is an open secret that the political leaders, representing different parties, have crores of bank account in different national and international banks, having millions of properties in various names.

Few years ago, it was felt that the backwardness is the only reason in northeast's tribal conflict and terrorism. To weed out this problem the then Prime Minister Atal Behari Bajpayee made a special grant for northeast. True, in some extent, underdevelopment is one of the root causes of the crisis in northeast. But it is not the sole reason of the crisis.

The Sukla Commission under the chairmanship of S.P.Sukla stated that there is a yawning gap of development between northeast and rest of the country. To bridge the gap it requires Rs. 93,619.01 crore in infrastructure in five to ten years gap. But it is impossible for the government to arrange such a huge fund within its limited resource and time.

The root causes of conflict lie somewhere else, apart from the remaining issue of underdevelopment.There is the problem of language autonomy, the problem of religious conversion and the problem of political and cultural identity. All these problems cannot be solved only by providing financial grants or through the pace of development. As mentioned, the problem of government corruption has to be addressed more seriously. No meaning to make such plans and programmes unless corruption is wiped out from the present political system otherwise .

To reduce the tension and conflict, government should move in the direction of negotiating the fundamental issues which generally creat the conflicts in northeast.

- Offer an independent representative organ with its own powers in the economic and financial fields.
- An autonomous administration.
- No discrimination against the tribal language.
- Confirmation of the freedom of association and assembly.
- Preference should be given to all tribal groups to present their cultural and social values.And it is the responsibility of government to promote their culture and social values.
- Government should set up schools and colleges at various tribal dominated areas without any discrimination.
- Government should facilitate the health-care infrastructure and provide adequate staff in their locality.

- All tribal groups should be given the equal opportunity in pursuing higher education and government jobs.
- Government should take the representatives of the tribal groups in major decision making process and held their views.
- It should try to build up the inter- community relationship among various tribal groups.
- Criminalization of public life, politics of vote bank, communal violence and corruption are major challenges before the governments.

(8) *Freedom of Religion*

Freedom of religion is in the provision the Constitution, and the government respects this right in practice. However, in some cases it does not act effectively to counter societal attacks against religious minorities.

India is a secular state in which all faiths generally enjoy freedom of worship; government policy does not favour any religious group. However, tension between Muslims and Hindus, and to an increasing extent between Hindus and Christians, continues to pose a challenge to the secular foundation of the state. In addition governments at state and local levels should respect religious freedom of each and every tribal group.

Although the law provides for religious freedom, enforcement of the law has been poor, particularly at the state and local levels, where the failure to deal adequately with intra-group and inter-group conflict and with local disturbances has abridged the right to religious freedom. In particular, some extremist groups continued to attack minority during the decade. In many cases, the government response was inadequate, consisting largely on statements criticizing the violence against minorities. With only marginal efforts to hold accountable those persons responsible, or to prevent such incidents from occurring.

State governments which are pledged to respect India's traditions of secular government and religious tolerance. However, political parties, links with extremist groups, that have been implicated in violent acts against minorities.

In the whole northeast, there were reports of attacks on minority groups. Legally mandated benefits are assigned to certain groups, including some groups defined by their religion. There are many religions and a large variety of denominations, groups, and subgroups in the northeast, but Christians, in some states (Mizoram – 85.73 %, Nagaland – 87.47 %, Megalaya – 64.58 % , Census report 1991) as dominant force of northeast largely take part in state affairs.

The Role of Religious Organisations

The current legal system accommodates minority religions' personal status laws; there are different personal laws for different religious communities. Religion-specific laws pertain in matters of marriage, divorce, adoption, and inheritance.

Missionaries and religious organisations must comply with the Foreign Contribution (Regulation) Act (FCRA), which restricts funding from abroad and, therefore, the ability of certain groups to finance their activities. The Government is empowered to ban a religious organisation if it has violated the FCRA, has provoked intercommunity harmony, or has been involved in terrorism or sedition. There is no ban on professing or proselytizing religious beliefs; however, speaking publicly against other beliefs is considered dangerous to public order, and is prohibited.

Government Policies on Refugees and Immigrants

On August 28, 2000, the Supreme Court gave the central government until January 2001 to repeal the Illegal Migrants Determination by Tribunal (IMDT) Act of 1985. The court ruled that the law, which is largely aimed at illegal Bangladeshi immigrants, is being applied only in Assam, and therefore is discriminatory. Bodo-Santhal ethnic clashes, which began in April 1998, continued throughout the year. More than 87,000 persons live under poor conditions in relief camps in Assam's Kokrajhar, Gosaigaon, and adjoining districts as a result of the ongoing violence between Bodos and Santhals.

The law does not contain provisions for processing refugees or asylum seekers in accordance with the 1951 U.N. Convention Relating to the Status of Refugees and its 1967 Protocol, nor is there a clear national policy for the treatment of refugees. The Office of the U.N.

High Commissioner for Refugees (UNHCR) has no formal status, but the government permits the UNHCR to assist certain groups of refugees (notably Afghans, Iranians, Somalis, Burmese, and Sudanese). The U.N. High Commissioner for Refugees, Sadako Ogata, visited the country on several occasions.The Government has not permitted the UNHCR to assist other refugee groups.

The government recognises certain groups, including Chakmas from Bangladesh. Many Chakmas from Bangladesh have been repatriated voluntarily, including all of the estimated 56,000 persons who had been residing in Tripura. Some 80,000 Chakmas are the permanent residents remain in Arunachal Pradesh and Mizoram. The Supreme Court has upheld their right to citizenship. However, the Supreme Court's order to extend citizenship to this group had not been enforced till date.

The Reang tribal group of Mizoram has been displaced due to a sectarian conflict, presently sheltered in 6 refugee camps in north Tripura.Conditions of these camps are very poor. Reang leaders in the camps say that their community will return to Mizoram if they were granted an autonomous district council, allotted a number of seats in the Mizoram Assembly, and granted financial assistance for resettlement. The Mizoram government rejected these demands and maintained that only 16,000 of the refugees had a valid claim to reside in the state.

On August 7,2000, following his meeting with Tripura Chief Minister Manik Sarkar, the former Union Home Minister L.K. Advani announced that an initial group of Reang refugees would be resettled in Tripura by October 31,2000 and the repatriation of the entire group would be completed by same year. However, NHRC members also visited Tripura to inquire the situation of the Reangs, by year's end, but the repatriation didn't take place.

The Right of Citizens to Change their Government

The Constitution provides citizens with the right to change their government peacefully, and citizens exercise this right in practice through periodic, free, and fair elections held on the basis of universal suffrage. The country has a democratic, parliamentary system of government with representatives elected in multiparty elections. A

Parliament sits for 5 years unless dissolved earlier for new elections, except under constitutionally defined emergency situations. State governments are elected at regular intervals except in states under President's Rule.

On the advice of the Prime Minister, the President may proclaim a state of emergency in any part of the national territory in the event of war, external aggression, or armed rebellion. Similarly, President's Rule may be declared in the event of a collapse of a state's constitutional machinery. The Supreme Court in May 1995 upheld the government's authority to suspend fundamental rights during an emergency.

The Constitution reserves seats in Parliament and state legislatures for "scheduled tribes" and "scheduled castes" in proportion to their population. Indigenous people actively participate in national and local politics, but their impact depends on their numerical strength. In the northeastern states, indigenous people are a large proportion of the population and consequently exercise a dominant influence in the political process.

The Inner-line Regulations enacted by the British in 1873 still provide the basis for safeguarding tribal rights in most of the northeastern border states. They are in effect in Arunachal Pradesh, Nagaland, Manipur, and Mizoram, but not in Tripura. In Tripura the tribal population has been reduced to 30 percent of the total population due to increased Bengali migration since partition.

These regulations prohibit any person, including citizens from other states, from going beyond an inner boundary without a valid permit. No rubber, wax, ivory, or other forest products may be removed from the protected areas without prior authorization. No outsiders are allowed to own land in the tribal areas without approval from tribal authorities.

The 1991 census, showed that 8.08 percent of citizens belonged to scheduled tribes. According to the Indian Confederation of Indigenous and Tribal People (ICITP), 80 percent of the tribal populations live below the poverty level. In May 1998, the NHRC established a panel to investigate the condition of the country's 20 million denotified tribal people, who in 1871 the British colonial government labeled as belonging to "criminal tribes". During the year, the panel prepared a report for the NHRC on their condition and advised the NHRC in other ways.

The colonial act listing these tribes was repealed in 1951, but the stigma remains and many of these tribal people still are discriminated against actively. The NHRC recommended that the "Habitual Offenders Act," aimed at the denotified and nomadic tribes, be repealed.

Despite constitutional safeguards, the rights of indigenous groups in the northeastern parts of the country often are ignored. Indigenous people suffer discrimination and harassment, have been deprived wrongly of their land, and have been subject to torture and to arbitrary arrest.

Such violations led to numerous tribal movements demanding the protection of land and property rights. The Bodo movement in Assam, Reang movement in Mizoram and Chakma movement in Arunachal Pradesh reflects deep economic and social grievances among indigenous people.

There is also the question of local autonomy in northeast. In Meghalaya tribal chiefs still wield influence in certain villages. The Nagaland government controls the rights to certain mineral resources, and autonomous district councils, in Tripura, Assam, and Meghalaya control matters such as education, rural development, and forestry in cooperation with the state governors.

The Question of Reang Repatriation

Reangs are suffering in refugee camps since more than 6 years in Tripura. More than 2000 people have died in various diseases, without any health care and basis facilities such as shortage of food grains and inadequate supply of drinking water. They have completed 6 years term without any adequate measures of food, drinking water, sanitation and education. What the minimum amount of food grains supplied by the centre is inadequate and irregular. The overall situation has posed a great threat to the entire Reang refugees. Government of Tripura made a clear strategy not to provide sufficient quantity food grains and other basic services like proper healthcare and education in which refugees are further victimized. This further violates the refugee rights and the schedule norms of UNHCR.

The Mizoram government engaged Bru National Liberation Front (BNLF) in its first round of talks to explore the possibilities of resolving the conflict unleashed in Mizoram. The subsequent discussions during 2001 and 2002 collapsed because of BNLF's special demands of involving the representatives of the Ministry of Home Affairs, or top officials of the Subsidiary Intelligence Bureau in bilateral talks. However, the Mizoram government did not accept these conditions, and it maintained that the issues to be discussed were state subjects.

The Mizoram government should realise that the demand of the BNLF, for third party involvement, is a reflection of its lack of faith in the Mizoram government's capacity to empathize with the needs and demands of the Reangs, whom the BNLF represent.

Unless each side understands the compulsions of the other side, no political solution can be reached through dialogue. The Mizoram government needs to understand that the Reangs, who are the second largest community in the state after the Mizos, and feel that they are educationally and economically backward, as compared to Mizos. Reangs want political empowerment through an Autonomons District Council (ADC), as well as reservation of seats in the state Assembly. So, instead of merely "joining the bandwagon" in holding peace talks, there is first a need to understand the raison d'etre behind the conflict dynamics generated by the BNLF. Unless the Mizoram government realizes the legitimacy of the demands of the BNLF and the Reangs, there is no point talking with terrorists.

The BNLF leaders also try to understand the political compulsions of the Mizo leaders. There already three ADCs of Pawi, Lakher and Chakma tribes exist in Mizoram. The addition of another Autonomous District Council (ADC) would increase the chances of political disintegration. Emerging from this political insecurity of the Mizo leaders is their conditionality that they would negotiate with the BNLF, only if the terrorist outfit renounced armed insurgency. The Mizo leaders obviously fear that if it accepts the demands of the BNLF, while it is allowed to carry on extortion and attacks on security forces in Mizoram, then the terrorist outfit may interpret it as a tactical victory.

But the very fact is that the two sides have managed to negotiating the problem,signifies a move towards reconciliation of contradictory interests may have started, and the possibility of a political solution has increased, provided the core problem areas are tackled headlong.

The intention of the central government even is not clear on the policy of Reang resettlement and repatriation. Government is not exerting adequate pressure to the Mizoram government for the early repatriation of the Reang refugees in Mizoram. Government is perhaps failing to put any pressure on Mizoram government may be because of Zoramthang's greater role in negotiating with the insurgency groups in northeast.He has been assigned to resolve the Nagaland dispute, held couple of discussions with NSCN (I-M) groups. Centre is looking for its greater successive role but dempened the Reang repatriationon on the other hand.The Reang problem is as important as the problem of NSCN (I-M) and others insurgent groups in northeast. The Reang terrorist group has clearly articulated that if the problem of Reangs is not solved within certain parameters they will be bound to take the underground activity. Presently BNLF militant group has totally maintained the silence and there is no more report of violence and attacks on human life.

Mizoram Chief Minister Zoramthanga made the commitments of solving the Reang problem, if militants surrender. BNLF militants surrendered officially,but government failed to maintain his commitment and it did nothing to resolve the Reang problem. Mizoram government, time to time, sitting with the surrendered militant leaders. But that did not progress the Reang sistuation. Mizoram government is saying that it cannot provide autonomous council and there will not be any reservation in Assembly for Reang leaders. This clearly shows that Mizoram government is not at all willing to solve the Reang repatriation. This political inability to resolve the 'Reang repatriation' will only provide the misery to the people of both sides. This should not be allowed to continue for a long period, the BNLF is fully committed to take up guns further and violence and insurgency may cripple any time in Mizoram.

Mizoram government cannot solve the problem alone for its internal disturbances and their is fear to lose the majority Mizo support. It requires centre's intervention and delivery of a neutral judgment on their repatriation. The best way is to find a appropriate solution and how Reangs interests and rights can be safeguarded through the provision of constitution. What is more required – is the regular observation of the NHRC to the Reang issues and apply its instrument for the Reang rights. Most particularly, NHRC has to be more instrumental on the early resolving of Reang refugees' problem.

The Lakhers (Maras) , Pawins (Lais) and the Chakmas were given the separate autonomous district councils at the time Mizoram was elevated to the status of Union Territory in January 1972. And, why the Reangs (Bru) will not enjoy similar rights? The demand of Reang autonomy cann't be simply weeded out or dismantled as because of the state's own internal factors.

According to the provision of the 5th and 6th schedule of the constitution, the demand for separate autonomous district council, and political representation is found to be genuine. The important issue here is to understand whether the migrated Reangs will be accepted in Mizoram. Does the government or Majority Mizos have the will? Can their aspiration and rights be fulfilled after repatriation? Otherwise some political arrangements may be made in between Mizoram and Tripura governments. If there are further risks involved in their repatriation in Mizoram, Reangs refugees may be integrated in Tripura state alongwith already existing large Reang tribal groups in Tripura. It is possible only when central government will make a blueprint on this issue in a very effective manner. Until their repatriation, it is suggested not to withdraw support both by Central and Tripura governments. After long years of staying in dilapidated condition, they became very weak both mentally and physically. Lost all their hopes, aspirations and mental balances; they are completely hopeless about their future. Majority of the refugees in camps become symptomatic in the fear psychosis of future threat perception. The refugee children are growing without any education, which is pushing them into more backwardness. Frustration is also rising. The present systems need to be overhauled more urgently. The following are the major obstacles of the Reang refugees and found inadequate by this anthor during his visit to the refugee camps.

(1) *Shortage of Relief Staff*

Government should deploy special and experienced relief distribution staff. In present system, the Relief distribution charge is given to local S.D.O office, whose responsibility mostly involved with the administrative works at Kanchanpur sub-division. In absence of adequate number of relief operation staff, the administrative system has been collapsed and even the relief distribution is not properly maintained and reported irregular.

(2) *Poor Facility of Drinking Water*

The Reangs settled at semi-hilly areas of Kanchanpur sub-division where there is always the shortage of drinking water. Geographically far an isolated place, with rest of the areas in Tripura, local administration is finding it difficult to supply pure drinking water. The existing installation of mark-ll 30 tube wells and construction of 16 RCC well could not meet the demand of existing 32 thousand population of Reang refugees. Almost half of the tube wells are not functioning; it has created huge water paucity in the refugee camps. And pure drinking water is a distant dream of the locality. The impure water intake has claimed many lives since 1997.

(3) *Shortage of Sanitary Latrines*

Almost 70 percent of the Reang refugees do not have sanitary larine facility. During 1998-99, 951 number of latrines were constructed at different camps and some constructions are going on. But the shortage of sanitary latrines in this thickly populated refugee camps has created an unhygienic and unhealthy atmosphere, all that affects to their healthy and normal living.

(4) *Inadequate Supply of Ration*

It is reported insufficient supply of ration in the camps, which is inadequate to meet the genuine needs of the refugees sheltered in six camps. Which need to be examined in oder to feed all the refugees. Presently government was providing 450 gms of rice per adult per day and cash dole Rs. 2.50 per day per adult, which was further demanded to increase up to rice 500 gms per day and cash dole Rs. 4.50 per day per adult respectively.

(5) *Need Permanent Doctors in the Refugee Camps*

Malaria, diarrhea and cholera that caught up Reang refugees at regular intervals and claim many lives. Earlier doctors were deployed to prune the disease. But government lifted the doctor services in the refugee camps. It created much worse than a congenial situation. For emergency health check up they have no option to get quick remedy.

(6) *Need Education Schools*

Government has not initiated to open schools at the camps. It was only through NGO initiative and presently Kalyan Ashram operates schools at the refugee camps. As a result many Reang youths become uneducated. It is reported that 5,412 minor children in the camps, mostly became uneducated and illiterate. This illiteracy will further push them into more backwardness. Government should take urgent steps to open up schools and try to readmit them for higher studies in Tripura or other states.

(7) *Government should Make Effective Strategy*

Government of Mizoram and Tripura should make an effective strategy to address the root causes of internal displacement. State governments should ignore their own political agendas and be less reactive on political issues and should take a proactive role for uplifting the rights of internal displaced peoples (IDP). Central government should also provide more attention to the internal displaced Reangs and other people in northeast. Non governmental organisations should be encouraged so that they can play more prominent role for uplifting their basis human rights. Reangs are suffering being the non-citizens of Mizoram. In order to support them, it is essential to improve the mechanism of better statistics and data need to be collected through surveys covering sex, age, and occupation. A system of national personal identification cards should be implemented. Displaced persons having lost their Ids during displacement would thereby gain easier access to the school system and to social services and constitutional rights.

APPENDIX

FRONTLINE

Vol. 15 July 18 - 31, 1998

SOCIAL TENSIONS

The Reang refugees

Reangs, who fled Mizoram in the wake of inter-community violence and are now housed in refugee camps in Tripura, face an uncertain future.

SYED SAJJAD ALI ***in Kanchanpur***

As many as 35,000 people of the Reang tribe, who have crossed over from Mizoram to Tripura since October last year following atrocities committed against them allegedly by Mizos, are stranded in eight camps in North Tripura. Their lives are full of uncertainties: a political solution to their problems is nowhere in sight and death and disease stalk the camps.

Enteric diseases have taken a heavy toll of the refugees - men, women and children - over the past two months. Officials of the Tripura Government confirmed 210 deaths. Relief workers said that a virulent attack of diarrhoea claimed an average of 15 lives a day since May 29 in the eight camps situated on the banks of the Deo and Longai rivers in Kanchanpur subdivision, some 220 km from Agartala.

The incidence of diarrhoea reached epidemic proportions in the second half of May. Enteric diseases are common in northeastern India. Conta-minated water and stale food are said to have caused the epidemic.

It was a nightmare for the refugees. Pintu Reang, 10, lost his father and sister within the span of a week. His mother too was sick. "If she dies," Pintu said, "I will be orphaned."

"The situation wo-uld not have worsened had the administration taken preventive measures at the initial stages," said Dr. B.C. Das.

member of a special medical team which treated about 700 patients. "There were only two doctors and a few bags of medicines to cater to eight camps," said A. Tuisarai Bru, vice-president of the Bru National Union (BNU), in the Gachiram Para camp, which is the biggest camp and which houses 18,000 refugees. However, the State Health Department and the North Tripura district administration acted after Chief Minister Manik Sarkar reviewed the situation at a high-level meeting. An anxious Chief Minister directed the agencies concerned to tackle the situation on a war-footing. He sent Health Minister Keshab Majumdar to the camps to supervise the functioning of the special medical teams that were sent out after the meeting. Later Manik Sarkar visited the camps.

The epidemic was finally brought under control, with medical teams serving patients round the clock. Refugee youth also extended voluntary service to the health teams.

Sudhir Sharma, Principal Secretary to the State Government, said: "We have also arranged to supply 40,000 litres of drinking water every day." According to him, the Tripura Government spent Rs.2 crores on relief work and the Union Government sanctioned Rs.1.2 crore. The Centre had directed the State to provide the same level of relief to Reangs as the Chakma refugees and promised to bear all the expenses, Sharma added. New Delhi spent about Rs.100 crores on the Chakmas over 12 years until their problems were solved through a political settlement in February last.

WHILE the refugees battled against heavy odds, the much-awaited talks between the Reang leaders and the Mizoram Government collapsed. The meeting was convened in Aizawl on June 11 at the initiative of the Union Home Ministry.

At the meeting, the BNU, the apex body of Mizoram Reangs (known in Mizoram as Brus), submitted a memorandum to Mizoram Chief Minister Lal Thanhawla, reiterating its demand for an autonomous district council (ADC) for Reangs in northwest Mizoram along the Tripura-Mizoram-Bangladesh border, under the Sixth Schedule of the Constitution. The other demands of the BNU related to the payment of compensation to Reang families that were affected by the inter-community strife.

Lal Thanhawla rejected the demand for an ADC and said later that the other demands would not be considered unless Reangs withdrew the "false allegations of killing, rape and atrocities". BNU president Soibanga Reang, who led the Reang delegation, refused to do so.

Lal Thanhawla argues that his Government's image has been tarnished by the "false propaganda" unleashed by Reang leaders. He says that Reangs do not inhabit a compact area in Mizoram and as such "they do not have the legitimacy to raise their voice for an ADC since most of them are aliens".

The Reang refugees arrived in North Tripura over the past nine months. The lack of initiatives by the Mizoram Government to get them to return to their villages and the refugees' stand that they will not go back unless their demands are conceded have worsened the problem.

Observers say that the traditional rivalry between Mizos and Reangs took a turn for the worse with Reangs demanding an ADC. Reangs, the second largest ethnic group in Mizoram, depend on *jhum* (shifting) cultivation for livelihood. They have a sizable presence in Mizoram - over 85,000 Reangs live across the three districts of Aizawl, Chintepui and Lunglei.

The BNU, formed in 1994 to "protect the rights" of the Reang community, floated the idea of an ADC at its annual convention in September last year, and this invited protests from several Mizo organisations. However, the BNU maintained that an ADC was necessary for the socio-economic development of the backward tribe.

Countering the Mizoram Government's stand, Bru National Convention of India (BNCI) general secretary Bimal Reang said: "Despite the fact that we constitute the second largest ethnic community in Mizoram, we have been denied all constitutional rights and civic amenities over the years." He said that Reangs had taken Mizo names and many of them had converted to Christianity, the dominant religion among Mizos. Tuisarai Bru said that "many of us adopted Mizo culture as well." He added that "our fate remained the same" in spite of doing all this.

Although Mizoram is India's second most literate state after Kerala, the literacy rate among Reangs is less than one per cent. The community has until now had only five graduates in Mizoram.

Tuisarai Bru stated: "Against this backdrop, we wanted to free ourselves from the domination of Mizos and raised our voice for constitutional provisions to become civilised citizens."

THE immediate cause of the exodus of Reangs to Tripura was violent clashes in the Mamith subdivision, a Reang-dominated area in northwest Mizoram, after the BNU raised the demand for an ADC. The Mizo Zirlai Pawl (MZP), a students' organisation, and the Young Mizo Association (YMA) vehemently opposed the demand. According to them, Reangs comprised less than 30 per cent of the population of the area and their demand was "part of a conspiracy to divide Mizoram."

Tension between the two communities escalated. Activists of the MZP and the YMA allegedly attacked Reang hamlets on October 13, 1997 and hundreds of Reangs fled the State. The situation worsened with the killing of a Mizo forest official on October 18, allegedly by Reang militants. Tuisarai Bru said: "After the body of the forest official was recovered inside the Dampa wildlife sanctuary, we were subjected to systematic attacks by Mizo youth. Five of our men were hacked to death, many were injured, at least 15 women were gangraped and hundreds of houses destroyed in a series of attacks." He alleged that the Mizoram police remained a silent spectator to the attacks.

The Mizoram Government repeatedly denied reports of atrocities on Reangs and stated that "a few thousand Reangs fled the State following some untoward incidents." The authorities also brushed aside reports that members of the Reang community were killed in the violence.

BNU leaders allege that MZP and YMA activists struck terror among Reangs, killing innocent people, torching homes and raping women. They claim to have listed 152 definite cases of rape and countless incidents of molestation. The Government in Aizawl described these allegations as false. However, trouble between the two communities continued, and so did the flow of Reangs to Tripura. By mid-June, according to official figures, 35,000 Reangs had taken shelter in north Tripura and still the influx remained unabated. A batch of some 7,000 Reangs arrived in the southwestern part of Hailakandi district of Assam during the same period.

Soibanga Reang insisted that the violence was part of a calculated move for ethnic cleansing. He alleged that first the names of 20,000 Reangs were deleted from the voters' list. "Next, there were state-sponsored atrocities."

At a health camp

Lal Thanhawla denied these charges but admitted that "some houses were torched by some Mizo youth." Making an indirect reference to the Bru National Liberation Front (BNLF), he accused a section of Reangs of taking up arms and "threatening their own people" to leave the State in order to manipulate the refugee issue and gain political mileage.

LEADERS of the tribal people in Tripura want the Mizoram Government to concede the demand of Reangs since an ADC is a constitutional provision that would help the allround development of the tribal people. Prominent tribal leader and Tripura Upajati Juba Samity (TUJS) MLA Shyma Charan Tripura said that Reangs were the most backward people among the tribal communities and it was the responsibility of the Mizoram Government to ensure their development through constitutional means.

"If the 60,000 Chakmas can have their own ADC in Mizoram, why not Reangs with a population of about 90,000?" he asked.

Reangs, one of the Tripuri clans, are considered to be the original inhabitants of Mizoram as the State was part of the Tripura kingdom until 1872, Shyma Charan said, quoting from a document. "In 1872, the British took control of the state from the Maharaja (king) of Tripura and it became a district of Assam," he added, brushing aside Lal Thanhawla's claim that Reangs were aliens. The community has a large presence in Tripura and the State's strongest insurgent group, the outlawed National Liberation Front of Tripura (NLFT), is dominated by Reangs. On several occasions in the past, Aizawl has accused the NLFT of providing arms and training to BNLF cadres to carry out an armed struggle against the State's government. What worries the authorities is the increasing restlessness among Reang youth as the Mizoram Government showed no indication that it is prepared to budge. The BNLF has been reportedly luring Reang youth from among the refugees for training in militancy-related activities.

The Tripura Government, however, has made it clear to the refugees' leaders that it will not allow any subversive activities on its soil.

A SIGNIFICANT allegation made by Lal Thanhawla is that the Rashtriya Swayamsevak Sangh (RSS) is "fanning trouble" in his State. The Chief Minister said that the RSS took up the cause of Reangs with the claim that they (Reangs) are Hindus and supported the false propaganda against his Government. He claimed: "Reangs are nomads and thus they are not Hindus, but animists." Lal Thanhawla has reasons to be concerned over RSS involvement in the problem.

The Vanavasi Kalyan Ashram, an RSS front organisation, has made an appearance at the refugee camps ostensibly to "help the distressed". It is also raising the Reang issue at various forums outside the region. RSS leaders under the banner of the Vanavasi Kalyan Ashram met President K.R. Narayanan in January and urged him to direct the Union Government to grant an ADC for Reangs in Mizoram.

As vested interests try to cash in on Reangs' problems, the refugees wait for a solution. Their leaders estimate that more than 500 of them have succumbed to disease, hunger and cold since they arrived in Tripura in October last. BNU leaders believe that the refugee problem, and the political crisis in northwest Mizoram, cannot be solved unless the political aspirations of the community are met.

THE WEEK

Oct 24, 1999

Strangers in their motherland Tripura: Reangs who fled Mizoram are nowhere

Tapash Ganguly, Ashapara

Ethnic conflict in Mizoram had driven minority Reangs to refugee camps in neighbouring Tripura two years ago. The refugees are now in conflict with fellow Reangs in Tripura.

Second-class citizens: Reang refugees in Tripura

The Mizos had forced the Reangs to leave Mizoram because the latter had demanded an autonomous district council. The Mizos prevented them from collecting firewood from the forests, denied them ration and kept Reang children out of schools. The government turned a blind eye to the ostracism.

In desperation, Reangs allegedly killed a Mizo forest officer in October 1997, thus provoking the Mizos to let loose terror in 100 villages in Aizwal district. Almost 35,000 Reangs fled overnight to Tripura.

The state government, which has been looking after the refugees, is now in a quandary. Tripura has a sizeable Reang population, mainly labourers in the orange orchards of affluent Mizos in North Tripura. "The refugees offer their services at low wages. This leads to intra-ethnic tension," said Kumar Alok, district magistrate of North Tripura, where all the six refugee camps are situated.

'Refugees offering to work for lower wages leads to intra-ethnic tension': Kumar Alok, North Tripura district magistrate

Besides, the refugees have started harvesting bamboo in the Kanchanpur forests which sustain the local tribals during the off-season in the orchards. The public distribution system in the state is also under severe pressure. The demand of rice for the refugees is almost half the entire requirement in the Kanchanpur subdivision. The situation becomes critical during monsoon when buffer stock can't be replenished easily. "There may be flare up if the refugee problem is not sorted out in the near future," said a Tripura government officer.

In November 1997, the home minister of Mizoram had visited the refugee camps and talked to the representatives of the refugees in the presence of Tripura home minister. "An atmosphere of repatriation was created and we felt hopeful when 3,000 refugees returned," said a bureaucrat. "But a large number came back with stories of Mizo hostility."

Mizoram is no longer willing to take the refugees back; their names have already been struck off the electoral rolls. The refugees are willing to go back only if they get an autonomous district council.

"We are second-class citizens there," said Hmangaisha, president of the Mizoram Bru Refugee Committee, Ashapara camp. "While Mizos get free education, health service and food, we have to pay through our nose. Even educated Reangs can't expect a government job. The very word Bru (Reang) is a taboo to the Mizos."

The government has so far spent Rs 18 crore on the refugees, and the burden is growing heavier every year. State officials see another cost, a dangerous one: they claim that some refugee camps are becoming a half-way house for insurgent groups.

THE ASSAM TRIBUNE

Guwahati, Wednesday, March 21, 2001

Only 10,000 Reangs bona fide residents

AIZAWL, March 20 — The State government claims to have completed the process of identifying the "legal" Reang residents of Mizoram and have placed the figure at a little over 10,000, reports UNI. With this, the Mizoram administration has literally rubbished the claims made by Tripura that over 31,000 Reangs living in the northern refugee camps belonged to the State. The announcement could have far reaching effects on the demographic profile of the region as Mizoram can now refuse entry to over 20,000 Reangs/Brus who were claiming to be residents of the State.

Placing the Reangs under two categories, the State administration claimed that while 10,142 refugees now languishing in Tripura refugee camps were the original residents of Mizoram, the rest had come from Assam, and parts of Tripura itself. According to the State government, while 8,396 Reangs were the residents of the Aizawl district, 1,746 belonging to the southern district of Lunglei.

Talking to UNI, Aizawl deputy commissioner C Ropianga claimed that the list prepared by the administration was based on records and not interviews. "Therefore, any Reang who could produce sufficient, documentary evidence on his citizenship would be added to the list," he said, adding that the administration had exhausted all means of identifying more people.

In August last year, Agartala had sent a list of 31,600 Reang residents of Mizoram living in refugee camps in Tripura. But, according to the State government, since the list did not mention the details of their villages, subdivisions, Assembly segments and polling station, the administration failed to trace their antecedents. The State Home department then referred the matter to Tripura asking for complete details of the claimants. During 1997-98, several thousand Reangs had fled to Tripura fearing repression from Mizos after a forest game watcher was killed by suspected Reang rebels in October 1997. The Mizoram government has so far maintained that the Reangs were forced to leave Mizoram by the Bru National Liberation Front (BNLF), a Reang militant outfit, demanding an autonomous district council for Reangs.

HUMAN RIGHTS FEATURES

(Voice of the Asia-Pacific Human Rights Network)

(A joint initiative of SAHRDC and HRDC)

B-6/6 Safdarjung Enclave Extension, New Delhi 110 029, India

In Mizoram fearing persecution from the ethnic majority Mizos, 15,000 to 50,000 Reang tribals have fled their homes since 1997 and found shelter in north Tripura, border villages of Assam and the Chittagong Hill Tracts of Bangladesh. In order to accelerate the repatriation process, the Tripura government discontinued food rations and medical services in some camps, causing at least 16 people to starve to death. At least 260 IDPs died as a result of inadequate shelter and unclean water, and around 1,400 reportedly became seriously ill. Additionally, displacement camps are susceptible to attacks and mismanagement, for which the National Human Rights Commission castigated the Mizoram government in a 1998 report.

It is clear that the Government of India must do more to protect the fundamental rights to life, security and dignity of the IDPs. Not only is current assistance and protection inadequate, government policy towards IDPs is inequitable, with Kashmiri Pandits receiving more assistance than their tribal Northeastern counterparts. Additionally, through the reduction of food rations and medical assistance, the government ignobly pressures IDPs to return to areas in which they feel unsafe.

To redress these problems the Government needs to develop a strong legal and institutional framework. The Guiding Principles on Internal Displacement, submitted to the UN Commission on Human

Rights in 1998, provide a sound ethical and pragmatic foundation for such a framework for IDPs. Drawing heavily from existing international treaties and conventions, the Guiding Principles include the rights of IDPs to assistance and protection without discrimination. The Constitution of India also affirms basic rights to life, food, and shelter. Together, these legal obligations can help structure a workable solution to these problems.

The Government should also strengthen its institutional capacity to assist IDPs by enhancing communication between vulnerable populations, their state governments and the central government. Displaced women, as household managers, must be involved in decision-making and assistance distribution to IDPs. Existing channels between displaced groups, administrations and security forces must be made more transparent in order to improve protection and prevent army abuses such as rape, arbitrary arrest and murder.

Finally, assistance and protection for IDPs in India must be supplemented by the vision and political will to bring lasting peace to the Northeast and Kashmir. Causes of conflict should also be addressed along with the symptoms of conflict such as internal displacement.

Future wars and internal conflict are likely to produce more IDPs than official refugees. In addressing the plight of IDPs in the Northeast and Kashmir, India can become an important frontrunner for future international law and policy developments.

THE ASSAM TRIBUNE

17 June 2001,

"Reang refugees in Tripura camps a miserable lot"

"Death stalks Reang refugees now sheltered in six camps in Kanchanpur subdivision in North Tripura district. During the last 10 days, 25 camp inmates died of malaria and gastroenteritis. The Reangs or Brus (now about 32,000 in all) who fled from neighbouring Mizoram following fierce ethnic clashes with Mizos in October-November 1997, are now a miserable lot. Uncertainty looms large over their future as several rounds of talks for their repatriation to Mizoram failed to yield any result. The Reang camps have become virtually death traps as diseases and malnutrition take their toll every year during this time. According to Tuichharai Bru, president of 'Mizoram Bru-refugee Committee," while 25 inmates, mainly children and old persons died of malaria during the last 10 days only, the figure stood at 250 in the last one year. He alleged that the civil and health administration failed to provide adequate medical facilities to the refugees. As the reports of deaths poured in from the camps, the administration sent medical teams to the affected areas. But shortage of medicines as well health staff has made their task impossible. The two doctors now present in the camps cannot cope with the fast deteriorating situation. Dr Shiromani Debbarma maintained that they could not arrest the occurrence of deaths for dearth of medicines. The inmates alleged that the civil administration did not take necessary steps for providing safe drinking water. For example, at Kashirampara camp out of five ring-wells, four are dried up while out of 13 mark-II tubewells, nine are out of order."

THE RELIGIOUS CONVERSIONS CONTROVERSY

45,000 Reangs hounded by Church to rootless existence

Sujit Chakraborty, Bishwa Hindu Parishad. www.vhp.org

Mizoram has shut doors to any possible return of over 45,000 Reang migrants who had to flee to neighbouring Tripura and Assam to escape mainly Christian missionary-backed atrocities and forcible conversions. Ironically, the national and international media and different political parties, which are crying themselves hoarse following clashes between Hindu and Christian tribals in Gujurat, have conveniently ignored the plight of the hapless Reangs tribals who are languishing in different makeshift camps of remote areas in Tripura and Assam.

Similarly, the rape of a nun in Jhabua and Baripada makes international headlines while rape of over a dozen Reang tribal women does not even prick the conscience of either the media or society at large. Leave alone a solution, even awareness of the plight of hundreds of tribal refugees barely surviving under inhuman conditions in camps for the past one-and-a- half-year is missing.

In fact, the root cause of the migration was the direct offshoot of socio-political consequences of mass conversion by Christian missionaries since the mid-nineties. Incidentally, Mizoram is a Christian majority State.

Large-scale conversions triggered ethnic conflict leading to migration of Reangs from Mizoram to Tripura and Assam, who have since been languishing in different make-shift camps and demanding safe return and rehabilitation to their ancestral homeland.

Bru (a derogatory term for Reang in Mizoram) National Union President Saibunga said in Silchar recently, "We are being persecuted by Mizos since we strongly opposed conversions. Mizoram is a Christian dominated State and they want everybody to become Christian. Even the Chakmas are facing persecution. Minorities are not at all safe in Mizoram. Since we raised our voice against the forcible conversions, we were driven away."

Reang refugees seem to be caught in a no man's land. Persecuted in Mizoram, which they call their homeland, they are now living under inhuman conditions in refugee camps in neighbouring Assam and Tripura since October 1997. And, there seems to be no end to their woes in sight, with the new Mizoram Chief Minister Zoramthanga categorically stating that Reangs are residents of Tripura and not his State. This declaration truly seems to have put the process of repatriation of refugees in a deadlock.

Mr. Zoramthanga's announcement has given a whole new dimension to the Reang problem. Reangs have recently been saying that they fled Mizoram as they were being forced to convert to Christianity in a Christian- dominated State. Thus, the problem has now taken up a communal colour, too, from being essentially an ethnic and political issue.

More shocking is that the refugees were also deprived of their voting rights in the last November Assembly elections in Mizoram. There are now 45,000 refugees in the two states - about 36,000 in Tripura and another 9,000 in Assam. They are uncertain of returning to their ancestral land and their only hope now seems to rest on the Centre to resolve the problem.

These refugees are living under terrible conditions in the make-shift camps. Last year, over 350 refugees had died following the spread of gastroenteritis and other diseases. Even now, paucity of medicines and food exist as quantities supplied by the camp authorities are not sufficient.

Sixteen-year old Maniram Reang, sheltered in a refugee camp in North Tripura, said, "Our condition is like that of animals here," adding, "We do not know what crime we have done to live away from our motherland in such terrible conditions in refugee camps."

Similar camps for refugees are located at Gachiram- para, Dosda, Anandbazar and Kanchanpur.

The major problem affecting the Reangs is fever along with skin diseases. According to a health worker in a camp, "Over 150 cases of fever are reported each day."

Though sometimes the Voluntary Health Association of Tripura distributes the medicines free, the quantities are not enough to overcome the extent of health problems.

The worse hit are the children, who have been deprived of a normal childhood. "We cannot afford to give our children even the basic needs of their life. When even we are leading a hand-to-mouth existence, how can we give the children a life that we would have wanted to?" said 70-year old Dhanu Reang of Anandbazar refugee camp. His wife echoes the sentiment, "How can these children grow as happy and healthy human beings? They have got a tough future in front of them." And she sums up the normal feeling in the camp, "I feel sorry for them." That's all they can do at this juncture.

But there are some signs of hope for their children. Purbanchal Vanvasi Kalyan Ashram, a voluntary organisation, has taken up the task of educating the children. The Ashram has recently appointed 19 educated youth from Reang refugees to run small schools. The teachers are also given a stipend of Rs. 400 per month for their efforts, besides books and papers.

The Vanvasi Kalyan Ashram volunteers are also active in Hailakandi district of Assam where nearly 9,000 refugees are sheltered in different camps including Gutguti, Riflemara and Ramnathpur, Dattapur, Bishurambasti.

The Ramakrishna Seva Mission, under the stewardship of Maharaja Khshayatananda, has also taken up the rehabilitation work in Hailakandi district about 60km away from Silchar town.

Displaced from their homeland, no matter how hard they wish, they are caught up in an unenviable situation. While the chief ministers of Tripura and Assam, Manik Sarkar and Prafulla Mahanta, have taken up the issue with the Prime Minister and Union Home Minister L.K. Advani, seeking Centre's intervention for an amicable solution to the 15-month-old Reang imbroglio, the Chief Minister of Mizoram is insisting that "Reangs are illegal refugees in Mizoram."

Talking to the Observer of Business and Politics at his Aizawl residence recently, Mr. Zoramthanga categorically stated that "the Reangs came to Mizoram from the neighbouring Tripura and they should go back to their homeland. There is no question of their return to Mizoram."

He also denied the report of forcible conversions and said that "we don't believe in forcible conversions."

In October 1997, there was a mass exodus of Reang tribals - who are treated as inferior by the Mizos - into Cacher district of Assam and North Tripura. The trouble started when the Bru National Union, the political outfit of the Reangs, organised its general assembly convention at Saipului in September, 1997 and raised a demand for creation of an Autonomous District Council for Reangs within Mizoram. The convention also demanded of the state government to make three Reang dominated assembly constituencies reserved for Reangs, much to the chagrin and consternation of majority Mizos.

According to Reang leader Ms. Ubati Reang, "The newly elected Mizoram coalition government has refused to concede the demanded Rs. 1 lakh as compensation for the displaced individuals. The state government and the Mizos volunteer organisations have openly announced that they will resist our repatriation move. And the displaced Reangs are now facing intolerable crisis. We are eagerly waiting for the Centre to resolve the issue."

She also spoke of maltreatment of Reangs by Mizos. "Over a dozen Reang women were allegedly raped by Mizos, besides burning down about 70 Reang huts by armed Mizos in November 97. This retaliatory action resulted in exodus of Reang refugees," she added.

REANG REFUGEES IN NORTH TRIPURA

REANG REFUGEES IN KANCHANPUR SUB-DIVISION

www.northtripura.nic.in/reang.htm

Due to ethnic disharmony and persecution by the Mizos. Reang Refugees of Mammit District and Longly District of Mizoram had to leave their places. These families started arriving in Kanchanpur Sub-Division of North District since 29-10-97 in search of safe shelter. These displaced reang refugees Leader have also submitted a Memorandum to the Government of India on 13-7-98 stating their grievances and demands. The issue of the Reang Migrants is sensitive and Multidimensional . the District Administration of North Tripura has been looking after this issue with utmost care.

UNI REPORT

www.newslinks.rediff.com/election/1999/sep/25poll2.htm

UNI over phone this morning reported that the Mizoram government has set up two polling stations along the Mizoram-Tripura border to enable the Reang refugees to cast their votes. They had been taking shelter in four camps in north Tripura since October 15, 1997.

The Mizoram government has set up the two polling booths following a direction from the Delhi high court for the benefit of the Reang refugees, who had fled to north Tripura from 10 Mizoram villages in 1997 fearing ethnic trouble after the killing of a Mizo forest official.

Kumar Alok said that the state government has made adequate security and transport arrangements for the Reang refugees to enable them to exercise their franchise in Mizoram, where election is now on for the state's lone Lok Sabha seat.

Transportation facilities had been made as a special consideration as the refugees had to cover a distance of 90 kilometres to cast their votes in the two polling stations.

The district magistrate has said that at present more than 31,000 Reang refugees were in the relief camps, but only 1198 of them were included in the Mizoram voters' list.

The refugee leaders had been claiming that the number of voters would be over 18,000. The Mizoram government had intentionally deleted the names of a large number of Reang voters from the electoral list, the leaders alleged.

The refugee leaders yesterday informed the district magistrate about their decision to boycott the election.

According to Mizoram Chief Electoral Officer L Tochhong, the Reang voters were identified on the basis of the electoral rolls prepared on July 21, 1999 by the Mizoram government.

Meanwhile, the police said that an influential students' body in Mizoram has protested against the setting up of the special polling stations.

The Reangs and their outfit Bru National Liberation Front had been demanding autonomous district council for the Reangs living in Mizoram.

The Mizoram government had rejected the demand on several occasions and had said that it would make efforts for the socio-economic upliftment of the primitive tribes.

The presence of Reangs in Mizoram was negligible till 1961 but there was a sharp increase in their population after 1971 which could only be attributed to a largescale migration from Tripura, a statement said.

UNI REPORT

June 9, 1998

www.indiabroad.rediff.com/news/1998/jun/09reang.htm

Centre to hold tripartite talks with Mizoram government, Reang refugees

A tripartite meeting between the Mizoram government, the Centre and the Reang refugee leaders would be held in Aizawl tomorrow to discuss the repatriation of about 30,000 Reang tribal refugees sheltered in north Tripura during the past eight months. Tripura's principal secretary Sudhir Sharma, who is looking after the relief and rehabilitation department, told reporters in Agartala this morning that a four-member Reang refugee delegation left north Tripura today to attend the tripartite meeting to be presided over by Mizoram Chief Minister Lalthanhawla.

The Reang refugees took shelter in many neighbouring north Tripura camps following ethnic violence in Mizoram villages in early October last year. Since then, the Tripura government has repeatedly requested the Centre and the Mizoram government to repatriate the tribal refugees. Tripura Chief Minister Manik Sarkar held meetings with his Mizoram counterpart and wrote to Prime Minister A B Vajpayee on the issue.

Reang, a primitive tribe among the tribals of the north-eastern region and mostly Hindus, are about 85,000 strong, living in the western part of Aizawl district in 75 villages and in a few hamlets of Lunglei and Chimtuipui districts in Mizoram adjoining Tripura.

They had been demanding an autonomous district council for them, a demand the Mizoram government has so far refused to accept.

MIZORAM ASKED TO TAKE BACK REANG REFUGEES

Headlines Vol. 2 Issue 29-30 Dec.7-Dec.21,1999

www.nenanews.com

The National Human Rights Commission (NHRC) has directed the Mizoram Government to take back an estimated 40,000 Reang refugees living in Tripura, and asked the Centre to play an active role in arranging their repatriation on priority basis, Home Ministry sources said. "The Reangs living in refugee camps in Kanchanpur sub-division of Tripura are lawful inhabitants of Mizoram and the State Government is obliged to take them back in accordance with the agreement made with the Union Home Minister in November 1997", the commission held.

After a meeting held recently by NHRC member Sudarshan Agarwal with chief secretaries of Mizoram, Tripura and Assam in Agartala, the commission said that the Mizoram Government should take all necessary steps to impart a sense of confidence and security to the refugees who fled the State in the wake of ethnic tension in 1997, sources said. It said dispute, if any, regarding the number of refugees could be resolved by joint verification at the camps by a committee comprising representatives of Tripura and Mizoram Governments and Union Home Ministry.

NHRC asked the Centre to play an active role in arranging repatriation of the Reangs to Mizoram in accordance with the decision taken in the meeting of Union Home Minister in November, 1997 and impart urgent attention to the safety and security of Reangs returning to their villages, they said.

MIZORAM ANIMUS PREVENTS REFUGEE'S INCLUSION IN POLL LIST

DH News Service, Agartala, November 9, 2003

Uncertainty is prevailing over the participation of Bru refugees sheltered in eight different camps of North Tripura in state assembly election to be held on November 20. The Mizoram government has ruled out the possibility of their inclusion in revised voter list. As many as 31,000 Bru refugees are living in Tirpura, out of which 4,065 had already attained voting age in 1997 when they came to Tripura.

The Bru refugee committee has already raised the issue with the election commission (EC) and sought it's intervention. The EC of India had then asked a team of Mizoram election officials headed by Chief Election Officer of Mizoram, Lalmalsawma to scrutinise the number of original Bru voters included in the Mizoram electoral rolls and the EC instructed the Mizo government to include the refugee voters in electoral rolls and set up polling stations in the refugee infested Kanchanpur area. Accordingly the state government took some steps but ultimately their attempts were foiled.

PARTIES PROTEST: All political parties and NGOs of Mizoram under the banner of "Save Mizoram Committee", an apex body that is fighting moves against the inclusion of Bru refugees in electoral roll, called for a state-wide general strike early this month. Official sources in Mizoram told Deccan Herald over phone that the state government has now withdrawn it's effort in regard to the revision of electoral rolls and the matter is still facing uncertainties.

Sources added, that the "Save Mizoram Committee" had defined its stand again by sending a letter to the chief election commissioner of India outlining the illegalities in the matter of revision of electoral rolls in Mizoram, which the committee strongly believes to be a violation of mandates of the "Registration of Electors Rules of 1960".

"The series of actions by the election commission authorities in Mizoram may result in a widespread public unrest leading to severe law and order problem," the memorandum maintained.

MIZO ADAMANCE: In its recent move to solve the dilemma the election officials of Mizoram once again scrutinised the number of eligible Bru voters and sent a revised number of eligible Bru voters to the EC of India which was again detested by the Save Mizoram Committee, who firmly believes that the process defied Registration of Electors' Rule 1960.

"The inclusion of eligible Bru voters in the electoral rolls of Mizoram cannot be detested, it is against the will of the law, what we stand against credentials of the inclusion of Bru voters from outside the state who were never citizens of Mizoram," said Lalrokhuma, chairman of the Save Mizoram Committee.

DECCAN HERALD

Wednesday, March 24, 2004

Postal ballot for Reang migrants

AGARTALA, DHNS: The Election Commission has granted postal ballot facility for Reang migrants who after being evacuated from southern Mizoram are staying as refugees in North Tripura.

The Commission declared them "notified class of voters" of Mizoram on Sunday and asked the Mizoram Government to issue postal ballot papers to them. About 31,000 Bru voters left Mizoram and took shelter in Tripura following ethnic clashes in October 1997.

Many could not cast their votes in the last election to Mizoram Assembly. Only 4,266 people cast their votes in the election as most of them could not be present at polling booths on time as they were staying in far-off places.

THE TELEGRAPGH

Wed, Nov 19, 2003

Refugee leaders dispute voter list

By Our special correspondent

Agartala, Nov. 18: The controversy over voting rights of Reang (Bru) refugees in Tripura for the forthcoming Mizoram Assembly election has taken a new turn.

Reang refugees from Mizoram have been sheltered for more than six years in six camps in North Tripura's Kanchanpur subdivision.

Their leaders have expressed resentment over the decision of the Election Commission as well as the Mizoram state election department to allow only 4,166 among 32,000-odd refugees to cast their votes in the forthcoming election to the Mizoram Assembly on Thursday.

Bruno Mesha, president of the newly-formed Mizoram Bru Displaced People's Forum, said over telephone from Kanchanpur that there were more than 15,000 genuine voters among a total of 35,000 refugees.

His stand was echoed by forum general secretary A. Sawibunga.

"During the revision of the electoral rolls, a 19-member team of the Mizoram election department, headed by chief electoral officer Lalmalsawama, visited the camps and arbitrarily deleted the names of a large number of bonafide voters and included only 4,166 names," Mesha alleged.

He added that even in the 1998 election, 15,800 inmates of camps were registered voters though they could not cast their ballots following intimidation.

He also disputed the number of inmates listed in official records, claiming that the Tripura government was saying there were 32,400 inmates but the actual figure was higher than 35,000.

Following directives by the Election Commission, the Mizoram government has set up altogether 17 booths at Kawanmun and Tuipuibari area on the border with Tripura to enable the 4,166 listed Reang voters to cast their ballots.

Sources in the election department here said North Tripura district magistrate B.K. Sahu would arrange to send the refugees on vehicles provided by the Mizoram election department. The Border Security Force would provide security cover to the voters.

Sources here described the decision of the Mizoram election department to allow some Reangs to vote in the election as a "welcome shift".

Over the past six months, all the political parties, social organisations and non-governmental organisations have launched an agitation to prevent Reang refugees from voting.

In a recent statement, Mizoram home minister T. Thanga said the entire state would have to be declared a disturbed area if the Reang refugees are allowed to exercise their franchise.

Sawibunga said the situation in at least 10 constituencies, where Reang tribal voters hold the key to the poll outcome, needs to be strictly monitored.

INDIA: COUNTRY REPORTS ON HUMAN RIGHTS PRACTICES - 2000

Released by the Bureau of Democracy, Human Rights, and Labor. Bureau of Public Affairs, U.S. Department of State, February 23, 2001

The law does not contain provisions for processing refugees or asylum seekers in accordance with the 1951 U.N. Convention Relating to the Status of Refugees and its 1967 Protocol, nor is there a clear national policy for the treatment of refugees. The Office of the U.N. High Commissioner for Refugees (UNHCR) has no formal status, but the Government permits the UNHCR to assist certain groups of refugees (notably Afghans, Iranians, Somalis, Burmese, and Sudanese). The U.N. High Commissioner for Refugees, Sadako Ogata, visited the country in May (see Section 4).

The Government has not permitted the UNHCR to assist other refugee groups.

The Government recognizes certain groups, including Chakmas from Bangladesh, Many Chakmas from Bangladesh have been repatriated voluntarily, including all of the estimated 56,000 persons who had been residing in Tripura. Some 80,000 Chakma permanent residents remain in Arunachal Pradesh and Mizoram; the Supreme Court has upheld their right to citizenship. However, the Supreme Court's order to extend citizenship to this group still had not been enforced by year's end.

Ethnic Chins are among the nonrecognized refugees in the northeastern states, particularly Mizoram. Chins and Chakma refugees have been targeted by student-led demonstrations protesting their presence in Mizoram. During the year, tensions between security forces and Chin National Force (CNF) insurgents operating in Burma allegedly resulted in the detention, interrogation, and expulsion of some persons associated with the CNF to Burma, where they credibly feared persecution. Human rights monitors allege that about 1,000 Chin refugees had been arrested in Mizoram and some 200 had been repatriated forcibly to Burma between July and September. According to one NGO, on August 3, a 25-year-old Chin refugee died in the Aizawl central police station, Mizoram (see Section 1.a.). An estimated 40,000 to 50,000 Chins live and work illegally in Mizoram.

Mizoram human rights groups estimate that some 41,000 Reangs, a tribal group from Mizoram that has been displaced due to a sectarian conflict, presently are being sheltered in 6 camps in North Tripura; conditions in such camps are poor and the Tripura government has asked the central Government to allot funds for their care. Reang leaders in the camps say that their community would return to Mizoram if they were granted an autonomous district council, allotted a set number of seats in the Mizoram Assembly, and granted financial assistance for resettlement. The Mizoram government rejected these demands and maintained that only 16,000 of the refugees had a valid claim to reside in the state. On August 7, following his meeting with Tripura chief minister Manik Sarkar, Union Home Minister L.K. Advani announced that an initial group of Reang refugees would be resettled in Tripura by October 31, and that repatriation of the entire group would be completed by year's end. However, while an NHRC staff member also visited Tripura to inquire into the situation of the Reangs, by year's end nothing had been done to repatriate them.

Section 3 Respect for Political Rights: The Right of Citizens to Change their Government.

The Constitution provides citizens with the right to change their government peacefully, and citizens exercise this right in practice through periodic, free, and fair elections held on the basis of universal suffrage. The country has a democratic, parliamentary system of government with representatives elected in multiparty elections. A Parliament sits for 5 years unless dissolved earlier for new elections, except under constitutionally defined emergency situations. State governments are elected at regular intervals except in states under President's Rule.

On the advice of the Prime Minister, the President may proclaim a state of emergency in any part of the national territory in the event of war, external aggression, or armed rebellion. Similarly, President's

Rule may be declared in the event of a collapse of a state's constitutional machinery. The Supreme Court in May 1995 upheld the Government's authority to suspend fundamental rights during an emergency.

The Constitution reserves seats in Parliament and state legislatures for "scheduled tribes" and "scheduled castes" in proportion to their population (see Section 5). Indigenous people actively participate in national and local politics, but their impact depends on their numerical strength. In the northeastern states, indigenous people are a large proportion of the population and consequently exercise a dominant influence in the political process.

In Assam the investigation into the 1996 murder of human rights monitor and journalist Parag Das has yielded no definitive information on the identity of his killer. The assailant allegedly was a militant who previously had surrendered and was supported by the Government (see Sections 1.a. and 2.a.).

In Assam's Chars River islands, some women work as prostitutes in exchange for as little as $0.23 (10 rupees). In 1998 prostitutes began to demand legal rights, licenses, and reemployment training, especially in Mumbai and New Delhi.

The Innerline Regulations enacted by the British in 1873 still provide the basis for safeguarding tribal rights in most of the northeastern border states. They are in effect in Arunachal Pradesh, Nagaland, Manipur, and Mizoram, but not in Tripura, in which the tribal population has been reduced to 30 percent of the total population due to increased Bengali migration since partition. These regulations prohibit any person, including citizens from other states, from going beyond an inner boundary without a valid permit. No rubber, wax, ivory, or other forest products may be removed from the protected areas without prior authorization. No outsiders are allowed to own land in the tribal areas without approval from tribal authorities.

The 1991 census, the last conducted, showed that 8.08 percent of citizens belonged to scheduled tribes. According to the Indian Confederation of Indigenous and Tribal People (ICITP), 80 percent of the tribal population live below the poverty level. In May 1998, the NHRC established a panel to investigate the condition of the country's 20 million denotified tribal people, who in 1871 the British colonial government labeled as belonging to "criminal tribes"). During the year, the panel prepared a report for the NHRC on their condition and advised the NHRC in other ways. Denotifed tribal peoples are tribal people The colonial act listing these tribes was repealed in 1951, but the stigma remains and many of these tribal people still are discriminated against actively. On February 15, the NHRC recommended that the "Habitual Offenders Act," aimed at the denotified and nomadic tribes, be repealed.

Despite constitutional safeguards, the rights of indigenous groups in the eastern parts of the country often are ignored. Indigenous people suffer discrimination and harassment, have been deprived wrongly of their land, and have been subject to torture and to arbitrary arrest. On July 4, a mob killed a 90-year-old tribal woman and set 16 houses on fire following the abduction of a nontribal youth from Futotip village in North Tripura. On August 17, a mob attacked Jatindra Kumr Jamatya, a tribal activist and member of the ruling CPI(M)in Nagrai, South Tripura.

Such violations led to numerous tribal movements demanding the protection of land and property rights. The Jharkhand Movement in Bihar and Orissa, and the Bodo Movement in Assam, reflect deep economic and social grievances among indigenous people.

There also is some local autonomy in the northeast. In Meghalaya tribal chiefs still wield influence in certain villages. The Nagaland government controls the rights to certain mineral resources, and autonomous district councils in Tripura, Assam, and Meghalaya control matters such as education, rural development, and forestry in cooperation with the state governors.

Religious Minorities

Other incidents affecting religious minorities during the year occurred in Tripura, at which Christian militants imposed bans on Hindu and Muslim festivals, and in Assam, in which Hindu concern over the continued influx of illegal Muslim immigrants from Bangladesh has grown over the past year (see Section 2.d.). On April 17, the secretary of the Noapara Baptist Church in Tripura was arrested with explosives in his possession. He allegedly was intending to take them to the NLFT.

National/Racial/Ethnic Minorities

The country's caste system has strong historic ties to Hinduism. It delineates clear social strata, assigning highly structured religious, cultural, and social roles to each caste and subcaste. Members of each caste—and frequently each subcaste—are expected to fulfill a specific set of duties (known as dharma) in order to secure elevation to a higher caste through rebirth. Dalits (formerly called untouchables) are viewed by many Hindus as separate from or "below" the caste system; nonetheless, they too are expected to follow their dharma if they hope to achieve caste in a future life. Despite longstanding efforts to eliminate the discriminatory aspects of caste, the practice remains widespread.

The practice of untouchability ("untouchables"—now called Dalits—along with tribals occupy the lowest strata of the caste system) was outlawed in theory by the Constitution and the 1955 Civil Rights Act, but it remains an important aspect of life. "Untouchability" refers to the social restrictions imposed on persons because of their birth into certain Hindu castes. Dalits are considered unclean by higher caste Hindus and thus traditionally are relegated to separate villages or neighborhoods and to low paying and often undesirable occupations (such as scavenging, street sweeping, and removing human waste and dead animals). Many rural Dalits work as agricultural laborers for higher caste landowners. By custom Dalits may be required to perform tasks for upper caste Hindus without remuneration. The majority of bonded laborers are Dalits (see Section 6.c.). Dalits are among the poorest of citizens, generally do not own land, and often are illiterate. They face significant discrimination despite the laws that exist to protect them, and often are prohibited from using the same wells and from attending the same temples as higher caste Hindus, and from marrying persons from higher castes. In addition they face segregation in housing, in land ownership, on roads, and on buses. Dalits tend to be malnourished, lack access to health care, work in poor conditions (see Section 6.e.), and face continuing and severe social ostracism. In contrast the highest caste, the Brahmin, with 3.5 percent of the population, holds 78 percent of the judicial positions and about 50 percent of parliamentary seats. NGO's report that crimes committed by higher caste Hindus against Dalits often go unpunished, either because the authorities do not prosecute vigorously such cases or because the crimes are unreported by the victims, who fear retaliation. In recent years, groups—including some that use violence—have organized to protect Dalit rights.

The Constitution gives the President the authority to identify historically disadvantaged castes, Dalits, and "tribals" (members of indigenous groups historically outside the caste system). These "scheduled" castes, Dalits, and tribes are entitled to affirmative action and hiring quotas in employment, benefits from special development funds, and special training programs. The impact of reservations and quotas on society and on the groups they are designed to benefit is a subject of active debate. According to the 1991 census, scheduled castes, including Dalits, made up 16 percent and scheduled tribes 8 percent of the country's 1991 population of 846 million. Christians historically have rejected the concept of caste. However, because many Christians descended from low caste Hindu families, many continue to suffer the same social and economic limitations that low caste Hindus do, particularly in rural areas. Low caste Hindus who convert to Christianity lose their eligibility for affirmative action programs. Those who become Buddhists or Sikhs do not. In some states, government jobs are reserved for Muslims of low caste descent.

The Scheduled Castes and Scheduled Tribes (Prevention of Atrocities) Act of 1989 lists new offenses against disadvantaged persons and provides stiffer penalties for offenders. However, this act has had only a modest effect in curbing abuse. The NCRB reported that 25,638 crimes against scheduled castes and 4,276 crimes against scheduled tribes were recorded in 1998. This compares with 27,944 crimes against scheduled castes and 4,644 crimes against scheduled tribes recorded by the NCRB in 1997. However, human rights NGO's allege that caste violence actually is on the increase.

INSTITUTE FOR CONFLICT MANAGEMENT

17 September 2001, www.ipcs.org

Bru National Liberation Front – Redrawing Faultlines in Mizoram

This is also the lesson which the Mizoram government should keep in mind as it engages the Bru National Liberation Front (BNLF) in the first round of talks to try and explore the possibilities of resolving the conflict unleashed by it in Mizoram. The BNLF—which is a terrorist outfit based in Mizoram, and operating in Mizoram, Tripura and Assam—sent a four member delegation to Aizawl on September 6. An earlier attempt to start negotiations in June collapsed because of the insistence of the BNLF that representatives of the Ministry of Home Affairs, or top officials of the Subsidiary Intelligence Bureau should be involved in the talks. However, the Mizoram government did not accept these conditions, as it maintained that the issues to be discussed were State subjects.

What the Mizoram government needs to realize is that the demand of the BNLF for third party involvement is a reflection of its lack of faith in the Mizoram government's capacity to empathize with the needs and demands of the Reangs, whom the BNLF represent.

The BNLF insurgency started in 1997, with the Reang Democratic Convention Party (RDCP) adopting a resolution demanding the creation of a separate Autonomous District Council (ADC) for the Brus (Reangs) in Mizoram in September 1997. This led to an ethnic backlash from the majority Mizo community, which feared the disintegration of their State, if such a demand was fulfilled. The Reangs have alleged that it was the Mizo Zirla Pawl (MZP), or the Students body of the Mizos, who combined with the police to start attacking the Reangs in October 1997. This led to a mass exodus of the Reangs from Mizoram to North Tripura district of Tripura and Hailakandi district of Assam. A large number of these Reangs, probably more than thirty thousand, still continue to live amidst inhuman conditions in six refugee camps in Kanchanpur sub-division of North Tripura district even today.

Inspite of repeated requests by the Tripura government and the BNLF, which claims to represent the cause of the Reang tribals, the Mizoram government has not yet undertaken the repatriation of these refugees. It is this recalcitrant attitude of the Mizoram government, which prevents the BNLF from trusting it, even as the two sides enter negotiations.

Unless each side understands the compulsions of the other side, no political solution can be reached through dialogue. The Mizoram government needs to understand that the Reangs, who are the second largest community in the State after the Mizos, feel that they are educationally and economically backward, as compared with the Mizos, and hence want political empowerment through an ADC, as well as reservation of seats in the State Assembly. So, instead of merely "joining the bandwagon" in holding peace talks, there is first a need to understand the raison d'etre behind the conflict dynamics generated by the BNLF. Unless the Mizoram government realizes the legitimacy of the demands of the BNLF and the Reangs, there is no point in talking with terrorists.

The BNLF leaders also need to understand the political compulsions of the

Mizo leaders. There already exist three ADCs of Pawi, Lakher and Chakma tribes in Mizoram. The addition of another Autonomous District Council (ADC) would increase the chances of political disintegration. Emerging from this political insecurity of the Mizo leaders is their conditionality that they would negotiate with the BNLF, only if the terrorist outfit renounced armed insurgency. The Mizo leaders obviously fear that if it accepts the demands of the BNLF, while it is allowed to carry on extortion and attacks on security forces in Mizoram, then the terrorist outfit may interpret it as a tactical victory.

But the very fact that the two sides have managed to reach the negotiating table signifies that a move towards reconciliation of contradictory interests may have started, and the possibility of a political solution has increased, provided the core problem areas are tackled headlong.

PTI, Aizawl

Thursday, January 31, 2002

TALKS BETWEEN MIZORAM GOVT, BNLF POSTPONED

Aizawl: The third round of talks between the Mizoram government and the Bru National Liberation Front (BNLF) on repatriation of Bru refugees lodged in camps in Tripura and other issues, scheduled for January 31, have been postponed as BNLF representatives failed to turn up.

Officials in the state Home Department said the next date would be decided by the BNLF and conveyed to the state government. The last round of talks was held in November.

The parleys between the two parties assumed added significance after the Mizoram government linked repatriation of the Bru refugees in Tripura camps to the laying down of arms by the BNLF.

The BNLF has been demanding a separate autonomous district council for the community by carving out the Western parts of the state.

www.Refugee/articles/india.org

Population growth led to competition for land and jobs, and to tensions among ethnic minority groups as well as between migrants and ethnic groups. Those tensions gave rise to ethnic and politically based insurgencies that have battled the Indian armed forces, attacked each other, and turned on civilian populations belonging to rival ethnic groups. The violence has caused widespread displacement.

Throughout the Northeast, conditions for the displaced remained poor during 2001. Violence and displacement continued in some areas, and no intergovernmental or international organisations were present. Many of the displaced lived in public buildings and makeshift shelters, with little health care and no access to formal education. State officials and local NGOs provided some food aid, but the assistance often arrived sporadically and was insufficient.

Ethnic conflicts in Assam State have left about 5,000 people dead since 1978. Clashes between Bodos and Senthals continued during the year, resulting in 40 deaths. In early June, the region's minister blamed the deaths of ten forestry workers on the National Democratic Front of Bodoland general strike to protest the continuing presence of the Chakmas, whom they still view as refugees from Bangladesh despite the ruling of India's Supreme Court that the Chakmas are Indian citizens. The All Arunachal Pradesh Students Union called the strike to pressure the provincial and federal governments to deport the Chakmas.

Bibliography

Ali, Syed Sajjad, "Social Tension: The Reang refugees", *Frontline*, Vol. 15(15), July 18 - 31, 1998

Amnesty International Reports, India. www.amnestry.org

Assam Tribune (The), "Reang refugees in Tripura camps a miserable lot" 17 June 2001, [Internet].

Assam Tribune (The), Guwahati, Wednesday, March 21, 2001

Barma, Suresh Dev, Tripura Adhibasi, *Jiwan-o-Sanskriti*, p. 40.

Basu, Durga Das, How the constitution has worked, chapter- 34. *Introduction to the constitution of India*, pp. 412 – 413.

Basu, Durga Das,Citizenship, chapter-7, *Introduction to the constitution of India,* pp. 73-74.

Bhambhri, C.P., One Country two System, , JNU, New Delhi, *The Statesmen* report, July, 13,2002.

Bhattacherjee, S.K., *Reang people of India*, Seagull Book, Calcutta, 1995.

Bhattacherjee, Suchintya, *Genesis of Tribal Extremism of Tripura*, Gian Publishing House, New Delhi, 1991, pp. 12-13.

Bipin Chandra, *India after Independence*, 1947- 2000, Mrudula Mukherjee, Aditya Mukuerjee, Penguin Books. pp. 103-104

Bru Refugee Committee, Tripura.

Chakma, U.K., Sub Divisional Officer, Kanchanpur, North Tripura, Government of Tripura.

Conditions for the Displaced. www.db.idpproject.org

Conflict-induced displacement in the Northeast, Training workshops on The UN guiding Principles on Internal Displacement, India report, p- 9, 28-30 November 2001.

Dainik Jugasankha, July 20, 2000.

Dalit Human Rights Defender Ruth Manorama speaking about the national campaign on Dalit H. Rights at Summit for H. Rights defenders held in Paris Dec. 1998.

Death Galore, *Northeast Sun*, New Delhi – August, 1998.

Diarrhea, malaria in Reang camps, 1817 died, *Dainik Jugasankha*, July, 3 2001.Guwahati.

Durga Das Basu, Fundamantal rights and duties, chapter –8, *Introduction to the constitution of India*, p. 90.

Food scarcity in Kanchanpur, 42 thousand Reangs in real trouble, *Dainik Jugasankha*, Guwahati, Assam. March 5, 2000.

Ganguly, Tapash, Strangers in their motherland, The week, Oct 24, 1999

Gastro breaks out in Hailakandi refugee camps, *The Assam Tribune*, July 10, 1998.

Global IDP project, Training workshops on The UN guiding Principles on Internal Displacement, *India report*, Page-2, 28-30- November, 2001..

GOI, *Annual Report, 2000.*

Hindu Frontline (The), 4 August 2001, *Hindustan Times* 2 August 2001; *NPMHR*, 5 January 2002

Human Rights at a Glance, *PRP Journal of Human Rights*, October-December,02 Anuran Chakma, Advocate, New Delhi .Pg- 38-39

Human Rights Features. (Voice of the Asia-Pacific Human Rights Network) (A joint initiative of SAHRDC and HRDC)

Humanitarian assistance, Global IDP project, Training workshops on The UN guiding Principles on Internal Displacement, India report, p- 7, 28-30 November 2001.

Hussain, S. Abid , Towards a new natioal culture, The National Culture of India.

In the rollback of Government policy, Reangs are dilly- dallying, *Dainik Jugasankaha*, June 14, 2001. Guwahati.

India: The Situation Of Human Rights, www.db.idpproject.org

Internal displacement in India: causes, protection and dilemmas by Mahendra P Lama, FMR 8 August 2000.

Internal displacement in India: causes, protection and dilemmas, in Forced Migration Review. *Review of the University of Oxford/Norwegian Refugee Council*, P Mahendra, August 2000, p.24-25. [Internet]

Internally displaced from Mizoram in Tripura: www.db.idpproject.org

It is impossible to bring back Reangs, if BNLF continues arm terrorism,: Zoramthanga, *Jainik Jugasankha*, 8 Sept. 2000.

Lalvihanga, P., Ministry of Infromation & Broadcasting, GOI, 1997. p. 11,12, & 18.

Lama, P., Lama of Many Hats, JNU, *The Times of India*. October, 21, 2002.

Living on the edge, Reang refugees in limbo, Surajit Thakur, *Eastern Panorama*, June, 1998. Guwahati.

Many Reangs Traces without children, Uttam kumar Shee & Mithulala Choudhuury, *Dainik Sonar Cachar*, December, 1998. Silchar, Assam.

Medhi, Shyambhadra, Parliament and Human Rights, President, Assam Institute of Sustainable Development, *PRP Journal of Human Rights*, October-December, 2002, pp. 23-31,

Ministry of Home Affairs, Government of India, (MHA-GoI), 7 August 2000, "Union Home Minister holds talks on the Reang issue" [Internet]

Mizoram ignores Reang return deadlines, October, 30,2000. *The Statesmen*. (Home Ministry press release, *04.08.2000* , Internet.)

Narayanan, K.R (President of India). Address to the nation on the eve of Republic day - 2000.

Negotiating Access: Northeast India, Paper presented at the Regional Conference on Internal Displacement in Asia. *Subir Bhaumik*, 22 February 2000,

Nehru, Jawarhal at Inaugural address of the seminar on Parliament Democracy on 25-2-1956.The philosophy of constitution, chapter-3,pg- 24, D.D.Basu, Wadhwa & Company, 18th edition.

Nehru, Jawarhal, LM C, Vol III, p. 150.

New plan of Mizo. Govt, not to return the Reangs, *Dainik Jugasankha*, January 20, 2002.

Non-Mizos are restricted to go outside, *Dainik Jugasankha*, May 25, 2000

Northeast India's Hidden Displacement, U.S. Committee for Refugees (USCR, p-1), 2000,

Panchyati Raj in Tripura with special reference to Panisagar community development block area, (Printwell, Rupa Books Pvt. Ltd, Tilak Nagar, Jaipur, 1993), pp. 35-36.

Protection from and during displacement, Global IDP project, Training workshops on The UN guiding Principles on Internal Displacement, India report, 28-30- November, 2001, P- 5

Reang autonomy heat on Mizoram government, *The Statesman*, June 10, 2001. Kolkata.

Reang People of India, Mizoram volume, Seagull Books, Calcutta, 1995, p. 157.

Reangs (Bru) demands separate identity. *The Sentinel*, Guwahati. March 28, 2000.

Reangs are unwilling to return if demands are not promised, *Dainik Jugasankha*, July, 1 2001.

Recruitment of minors and forced recruitment, Global IDP project, Training workshops on The UN Guiding Principles on Internal Displacement, India report, p- 6, 28-30- November, 2001.

Refugee problem may invite terrorism, *Dainik Jugasankha*, April 8, 1999.

Resentment over lifting forces from Reang areas. *Dainik Jugasankha*, May, 16, 2000.

Role of judiciary, PIL and media, p- 33 IIHR.

Rs. 22 Crore granted for Reang refugee camps, *Dainik Jugasankha,* 16 July, 2000.

Saha, K.C., 2000, p.7-8, UN Guiding Principles on Internal Displacements: A Case Study of Internally Displaced Reangs of Mizoram in North-Estern India, Views expressed in this paper are the author's personal [Internet]

Shee, Uttam Kumar and Mithulala Choudhuury, "Many Reangs Traces without children", *Dainik Sonar Cachar*, December, 1998. Silchar, Assam.

Shing, K.C., *Rajmala*, Akshar, Agartala, 1997 .

Shing, K.S. (Ed.), *People of India*, *Mizoram*, Vol 34.

South Asia Human Rights Documentation Centre (SAHRDC), 16 March 2001, No Refuge: the Plight of Conflict-Induced Internally Displaced Persons in India, [Internet].

Speech of Vice President, *ibid*, The philosophy of constitution, chapter-3, pp. 24, D.D. Basu, Wadhwa & Company 18th edition.

Tarkunde, V.M., Need for People Power, Senior Advocate, Supreme court, *The Statesmen*, 27 October, 2002.

Thakur, Surajit, "Living on the edge, Reang refugees in Limbo", *Eastern Panorama*, June, 1998, Guwahati.

Thousand Reang Refugees in absence of Food. *Dainik Jugasankha*, June, 1999.

Times of India, 4 August 2001, "Centre's assurance on Bru/Reangs problem" [Internet].

Trouble in return to Mizoram, November, 4, 2000. Guwahati.

U.S. Committee for Refugees (USCR), June 2001, *World Refugee Survey 2001* [Internet].

U.S. Department of State, February 2001, 2000 Country Reports on Human Rights Practices [Internet].

UN Guiding Principles on Internal Displacements: A Case Study of Internally Displaced Reangs of Mizoram in North-Estern India, K.C.Saha, (2000 p.11) 2000, Views expressed in this paper are the author's personal views and not the view of the, Government of India.

UNI report / www.newslinks.rediff.com.

USCR 2001 p.157 & USCR 2003, India.

www.db.idpproject.org.

www.Refugee/articles/india.org.

www.satp.org [Internet].

Index